The Relations of the Federal Government to Slavery

Delivered at Fort Wayne, Ind
October 30th 1860

by

Joseph Ketchum Edgerton

ISBN: 978-1-63923-221-5

Printed: May 2022

Cover Art By: Amit Paul

Published and Distributed By:
Lushena Books
607 Country Club Drive, Unit E
Bensenville, IL 60106
www.lushenabooksinc.com/books

ISBN: 978-1-63923-221-5

THE RELATIONS OF THE FEDERAL GOVERNMENT TO SLAVERY

SPEECH

OF

JOSEPH K. EDGERTON.

Delivered at Fort Wayne, Ind., October 30th 1860.

"The constitution which we now present is the result of a spirit of amity, and of that mutual deference and concession which the peculiarity of our political situation rendered indispensible." *George Washington, President of the Federal Convention of 1787 to the President of Congress.*

PREFACE.

The publication at this time of a speech of the Presidential Canvass of 1860, may seem uncalled for, and be imputed to other than the motives that influence me. I nevertheless submit it to the candid consideration of the public, and especially of such as having heretofore entertained wrong views on the chief question involved in the canvass of 1860 and the position of the lamented Douglas, may desire truthful information. The speech at the time of its delivery was intended as a vindication of that noble-hearted, but then much-abused and misrepresented patriot. The grave of Douglas now shields him from the shafts of partisan animosity. Even his enemies concede, that in his last and self-sacrificing efforts to unite the Democracy of the North in support of an insulted government and outraged constitution, he earned the meed due to eminent patriotism. A perusal of the following pages may, perhaps, convince some, before doubting, that Douglas was as wise a statesman and as true a patriot in November, 1860, as he was in May, 1861, when the people of Chicago with one accord united in a grand ovation to do him honor, not as a partisan leader, but as a pillar and hope of the Republic in its day of mortal peril. If what I have written shall induce but even a few candid men to think better of the departed Douglas, as a statesman and patriot, than they were wont to think, I will be more than rewarded for my own labor in his vindication. But I have other motives than this.

The time is not far distant, and I would gladly accelerate its advance, when the conservative sentiment of the nation will revive and have utterance, and demand the re-enthronement of the spirit of compromise and peace—the guardian genius of the unity of the nation. Men of extreme and violent opinions, both North and South, whose fanaticism, folly and ambition have brought our great American Republic to its present sad estate, must give way before the incoming tide of a just public opinion on the relations of the Federal government to slavery. The people of the United States have neither the heart nor the means for a protracted warfare with each other in regard to negro slavery. The war is mainly the result of misunderstandings and erroneous opinions in both the slaveholding and non-slaveholding sections of the Union, which dispassionate investigation will remove. When the deluded men of the South shall come to understand by abundant evidence, which the good sense and patriotism of true Union men will furnish, that the spirit of the war on the part of the loyal States is one springing not from hatred to the Southern people and their institutions, but from earnest love of the Federal Union, and a determination to defend and re-establish it in all the integrity of its principles, they will gladly return to their [Pg 4]first love and welcome the protection of the banner which has ever been the symbol of the power and glory of the United American people. If, however, the war on the part of professedly loyal men shall be guided by any other feeling than love for the Union and a sacred regard for all the obligations of its Constitution, the preservation of the Union will be impossible. The non-slaveholding States may, perhaps, bind the seceded States to them by the stern power of military subjugation, as Poland is bound to Russia, or Hungary to Austria, but the subjugation of one section of the Republic by another will never unite their people in the fraternal bonds of a true Federal Union.

The traditions and historic glory that surround the Federal Government as our fathers formed it, are yet dear to the hearts of the whole American people. That government still belongs to them—it is their heritage, and they, I trust, will yet restore and preserve it. The horoscope of the future daily brightens with hopeful signs, not the least of which is the fact that the President of the United States, who was elected to his high office upon a declaration of political principles logically involving the extermination of slavery as existing in fifteen States of the Federal Union, and which could not therefore be carried out without making the Union "a divided house," has himself become the supporter of a constitutional and conservative policy in regard to slavery. Let us thank God and take courage. If the government will but stand firmly on constitutional ground, we will not despair of the Republic.

It is also due to truth to say that one object I have in the present publication is to disabuse the minds of some of my fellow-citizens, whose good opinion I value, who have been misled by false statements charging me with sympathy with the Southern rebellion. The opinions now published were the result of patient investigation, and are still held with earnest conviction, confirmed by the events of the past year. Of their justice and patriotism, and whether or not they are the opinions of a sympathizer with rebellion, candid men will judge.

The speech is published with a few verbal alterations, as it was delivered, for the reason that in that form its true spirit can best be understood. Due allowance will therefore be made for its style, which is that of a popular address.

JOSEPH   K.   EDGERTON.

Fort Wayne, Ind., December, 1861.

[Pg 5]

SPEECH

Fellow-Citizens:—In early youth, almost in boyhood I may say, I attached myself to the Whig party. It was a conservative, rather than a progressive party, but it was one of noble principles and aims, and it had noble leaders, the greatest of whom now sleep in death. It was, and therefore I loved it, eminently a party for the Union and Constitution. It was a *national*, not a *sectional* party.

With the death of Webster and Clay, the Whig party, like a headless army, was broken and dispersed. Its victories and defeats are alike things of the past. Its history is written in the annals of the nation. The question of its patriotism is enrolled in the Capitol. Posterity will do it justice.

Bound by no party ties, I appear before you neither as a partisan nor a politician, but as an American citizen, to state freely my views upon the great political question that agitates our country and threatens its national existence, and to give you the reasons which constrain me to sustain Stephen A. Douglas and the National Democratic party, which he leads, in the presidential election near at hand, and I trust I will have your patient and candid attention.

The Federal government, under the existing Constitution of the United States, went into operation on the 4th of March, 1789, under the administration of George Washington as first President. It is seventy-one years since that event. During that period the number of the States has increased from thirteen to thirty-three, and another will soon be added to the number when Kansas, now waiting at the door of the Union with a republican and a free[Pg 6] Constitution, shall come in "on an equal footing with the original States in all respects whatsoever."

When the Constitution was adopted, the area of the United States was 820,680 square miles. At the present time that area has been increased to 2,963,666 square miles, or, I may say 3,000,000 of square miles—a territory ten times as large as that of France and Great Britain combined, and equal in extent to the empire of the Romans, or of Alexander.

At equal pace with the expansion of our territory has moved on and spread out the tide of human life, bearing on its bosom the religious faith of the christian, and the laws and institutions of the Celtic and German races purified by christianity and the love of freedom.

At the first census in 1790, the population of the United States amounted to within a fraction of 4,000,000 of people. In 1860 it will reach, if not exceed 30,000,000, and it is no vain boast to say, that in no other nation of equal population, is there so much of individual freedom, or so large an aggregate of rational, substantial, human happiness.

Such are the fruits of over seventy years trial and experience of the Federal Union and Constitution, and the heart of every true American patriot swells with a just and noble pride as he contemplates them, and more than this, it swells with an earnest longing—an ardent desire—that prompts him as he looks into the future, to breathe to the Sovereign Ruler of the Universe, the prayer—"God save the Union and the Constitution!"

No American heart that honors God, and truly loves America and the human race, has ever yet dared to think, much less to say, of the Constitution of the United States, as William Lloyd Garrison has said, "*It is a covenant with death and an agreement with hell.*"

The United States embrace a territory not touching either extreme of torrid heat or artic cold, but within those extremes—various in soil, in climate, in productions—a land we may say in the oriental style of Scripture language, "flowing with milk and honey," "a land of corn,[Pg 7] and wine and oil," fitted by Providence for the home of races of differing constitutions, habits, capacities and pursuits; and practically we know, that within our borders we have alike the European, the Asiatic, the aboriginal American and the African races, with all their strongly marked constitutional peculiarities; but our system of State and Federal Government can give to each race the measure of power and protection due to each.

The admirer of natural scenery, who from some commanding point of view, surveys an expanse of mountain and valley, and plain and lake and river, clothed in the summer sunlight, does not pause and check his pleasing and elevated emotions, to note with cynical eye, each stagnant pool, or noxious weed, or unsightly decaying tree that may lie within the limits of the noble vision. He rather admires the harmony and beauty of the whole, though he may know that there are within the scene before him imperfect, unbeautiful and unwholesome things. Such is the feeling of the patriot of well-balanced mind, when he contemplates the Union and the Constitution as they are. While he knows the imperfection of all work of human hands, he accepts and admires in the political work of our fathers, the grandeur and symmetry of the whole, and will not condemn or destroy it because it is not in all its parts a perfect work.

But such is not the feeling of every American mind. There are men assuming to be philosophical and practical statesmen—men who rank with a great political party as their representative men, who in all their views and studies of the American Union, see only or chief of all, "*the mean and miserable rivulet of black African slavery, stealing along turbid and muddy, as it is drawn from its stagnant sources in the Slave States.*" I quote the language of William H. Seward, in his speech at Chicago on Oct. 2d, 1860.

This Republican statesman, familiar with the pages of history, which teaches him that the rivulet of domestic servitude has run among the nations almost coeval with the stream of time; familiar by personal observation with the[Pg 8] aspect and condition of the civilization of Europe, where constitutional freedom is almost unknown; familiar also with the history, the institutions and the society of every portion of the American Union, and with the blessings which that Union, above all other systems of government the world has ever known, confers upon its people; sees all the glories of the Union dimmed, all its harmony destroyed, all its substantial benefits turned like Dead sea fruit to ashes and bitterness, when he beholds "the mean and miserable rivulet of black African slavery, stealing along turbid and muddy from its stagnant sources in the Slave States."

With this *one idea* ruling his mind, Mr. Seward labors in the Senate and before the people with all the learning and ability he possesses to rouse one half of the nation against the other to dam up, dry up or blot out "this mean and miserable rivulet." From Boston to Kansas, like another Peter the Hermit, he preaches a crusade against the institutions and people of the Southern States. He proclaims an irrepressible conflict between free labor and slave labor, between Free States and Slave States, between white suffrage and equality and black suffrage and equality, and he utters as he goes the atrocious sentiment, not of the statesman, but of the demagogue, "*Henceforth I put my trust not in my native countrymen, but I put it in the exile from foreign lands.*" I, the oracle of the Republican party, in effect says Mr. Seward, will not trust as the conservators of the American principle of freedom and the American system of free government, the sons of the men who fought the battles of American Independence, but I and they will trust the exiles from foreign lands—from Europe, from Asia and from Africa, to establish here upon the battle fields, rich with the blood of our fathers, the principles of universal suffrage and universal equality.

Mr. Seward hangs out the signal of uncompromising conflict. This, in effect, if not in words, says he, is the Holy Land of freedom and universal equality. Infidels and barbarians possess it in all its Southern borders, and[Pg 9] hold there black christians their coequals in all the rights of men in an inhuman bondage. Let us then by the aid of the exiles from foreign lands overcome the infidels and barbarians, and plant in all that fair domain the standard of the higher law, of universal suffrage and universal equality; and forthwith all through the North, Republican *Wide-Awakes* muster their forces for this great political crusade. I am drawing no fancy picture. What I say is but a legitimate comment upon the language of Mr. Seward in his Chicago speech, already referred to, and in other speeches he has made during his recent pilgrimage through the North-west. Mr. Seward is the self-constituted exponent of the *higher law* in its application to political parties and measures, and to Constitutions and systems of government, but in his pursuit of one idea, he seems to forget that the sacred volume to which we all look as the source of our best and truest knowledge of the will and purposes of Providence concerning man, if it clearly reveals to us any thing, clearly reveals this fact, which all human history confirms: that man is not a perfect being; that this earth is not a perfect state; that disorder, and imperfection, and inequality, and change must ever pervade it, and mark all human institutions. This earth and its mortal life is but the threshhold—the vestibule of human destiny—that reaches far into the eternal ages.

Believe, as he may, in human equality or in the perfectibility of humanity, no such theory has ever yet been realized, nor will it ever be realized in this probationary state of man. Philosophy may teach—political constitutions may declare, and political parties may attempt to enforce as a practical truth, that all men are equal. No such theory will ever find a perfect realization in any system of human government.

In his speech at Chicago, before referred to, Mr. Seward vauntingly asserts, as the idea or creed of the Republican party, as if to that party alone were committed the oracles of freedom—"That civilization is to be maintained and carried on upon this continent by Federal States, based upon the principles of free soil, free labor, free speech,[Pg 10] equal rights and universal suffrage." I pause but a moment here to note the pregnant meaning of this authoritative declaration of the representative man of the Northern sectional party. It means no less than that there shall be no Federal States on this continent where free soil, free labor, free speech, equal rights and universal suffrage shall not prevail. In other words it means that domestic servitude as now known in the Southern States of the American Union, *shall be abolished*, and that there shall be equal rights and universal suffrage among all the races who may inhabit the American continent. Herein is the end or ultimate goal of the higher law of Mr. Seward, and its coadjutor, "the irrepressible conflict."

Conceding that all these ends shall have been attained and African slavery forever blotted out, still will the doctrine of human equality, which lies at the base of the whole abolition movement in this country, be as far from its perfect realization as now, for the reason that it is not the will of Providence that such a doctrine can ever support a permanent system of human society; and yet, because of its supposed conflict with this utopian theory of equality, it is, that the Federal Constitution, which has been called by George Washington "the palladium of American liberty," has been pronounced by the radical apostle of abolition, "a covenant with death and an agreement with hell."

In pursuit of this delusive theory of equality and universal suffrage, the masses of the Republican party, who would deem it an insult to be charged with entertaining the traitorous sentiments of Garrison, are inaugurating and sustaining a political movement, the inevitable result of which will be to destroy the Union and Constitution as they are. That the abolition of slavery is the necessary logical result and end of the political doctrines of Mr. Seward, no man who understands the force of language can deny, and until it shall have been fully explained how this end is to be attained consistently with the peace, the safety and constitutional rights of the slaveholding States, and how we are to deal with the millions of the African race,[Pg 11] who by the establishment of free labor, free speech, free soil, equal rights and universal suffrage, are to become the peers of their masters and of each and every one of us, I shall fail to believe that the abolition of slavery by any Federal action can coexist with the American Union under its present Federal Constitution.

I shall not pause now to speak in detail as to what are to be the fruits of the irrepressible conflict, nor shall I stop to inquire as to the purity or sincerity of the motives of Mr. Seward and his compeers in their crusade. When the christian crusaders of the middle ages precipitated the hosts of Europe upon Asia, the weary, wayworn soldiers of those countless hosts, as they traversed the burning sands of Syria, doubtless thought they were doing God service—their cause in their minds, was the cause of christianity and of humanity, and as Godfrey of Bouillon set the standard of the cross upon the walls of Jerusalem, recovered from the power of the infidel Moslem, he was ready like Mr. Seward, when he contemplates the results of the repeal of the Missouri compromise in the victories of the Republican party, to take up and exult in the song of Miriam, the prophetess. But as history proves in the case of the old crusades, so will it prove in the case of the crusade of abolition, that any premature attempt by material or political armaments to forestall and hurry on the great purposes and movements of Providence, cannot succeed. History tells us the result of the crusades.

"Every road leading to Palestine was drenched with blood, and along its dreary track lay scattered at no distant intervals the skeletons and the wrecks of nations. After four years of toil and misery and victory, Jerusalem was conquered by the crusaders; but as their conquests were not the work of wisdom and prudence, but the fruit of a blind enthusiasm and an ill-directed heroism, they laid the foundation of no permanent settlements, and in fact soon melted away like frost-work in the sun."

For seven hundred years since the crusades to free the[Pg 12] christian people of Asia from Moslem rule, that rule has been maintained in all its despotic power.

When will men learn by severe experience that political and religions ideas have conquered more in defence than in offence and aggression, and that reason is the true leader of ideas, and the paths of peace their certain way to victory?

In this one idea then of "black African slavery," as Mr. Seward calls it, we have reached the central fact, or as Abraham Lincoln would say, "*the particular spot*" upon which sectional parties are staking the destiny of the American Union. All other political questions have sunk to insignificance when compared with this. It would seem as if reckless men were determined that from "this mean and miserable rivulet," are to go out the poisonous waters that shall blast the fair face of this promised land of freedom.

"Slavery agitation, in my opinion," says Abraham Lincoln, "will not cease until a crisis has been reached and passed. 'A house divided against itself cannot stand.'" We are now in the midst of that crisis. It is the pendency of that crisis which has prompted me to address you to-night. For the first time in the history of the government, we have the spectacle of purely sectional parties struggling for the control of the Federal government, each determined to warp and bend to its own sectional end, the Constitution and power of the Federal Union. Never before could patriotic citizens so earnestly lay to heart the counsel of Washington to avoid the formation of sectional parties.

On the 17th of September, 1796, exactly nine years after he, as President of the Convention and Deputy from Virginia, had signed his name to the Federal Constitution, Washington thus addressed his fellow-citizens:

"The unity of government which constitutes you one people is now dear to you. It is justly so; for it is a main pillar in the edifice of your real independence, the support of your tranquillity at home, your peace abroad, of your safety, of your prosperity, of that very liberty which you so highly prize. But as it is easy to foresee that from different[Pg 13] causes and from different quarters, much pains will be taken, many artifices employed to weaken in your minds the conviction of this truth—as this is the point in your political fortress against which the batteries of internal and external enemies will be most constantly and actively (though often covertly and insidiously), directed, it is of infinite moment that you should properly estimate the immense value of your National Union to your collective and individual happiness; that you should cherish a cordial, habitual, and immovable attachment to it,—accustoming yourselves to think and speak of it as of the palladium of your political safety and prosperity; watching for its preservation with jealous anxiety; discountenancing whatever may suggest even a suspicion that it can in any event be abandoned; and indignantly frowning upon the first dawning of every attempt to alienate any portion of our country from the rest, or to enfeeble the sacred ties which now link together the various parts."

Fellow-Citizens, the portentous evil which Washington thus deprecated in his Farewell Address to the people of the United States is now upon us. I repeat we are in the midst of the crisis of sectional parties. How shall it be passed, so that the Union shall not fall?

It seems to me that no man who knows our history, who understands truly the genius of our people, and who understands also the principles upon which the Union and the Constitution are based, can fail to believe that it is not by the conflict of sectional parties and their triumph, but by the defeat of sectional parties by a stronger and more patriotic national party, that the divided house can be reconciled and the house itself made to stand in safety. The safety of the Union depends upon maintaining the Federal government in the hands of a national party, which shall carry out the spirit of the Federal Constitution. A solemn responsibility rests upon every citizen in this regard.

I propose then to inquire—

1st—What is the true spirit of the Constitution, and what[Pg 14] the true policy of the Federal government on the subject of slavery? and,

2d—How do the parties and the candidates now before the people stand in regard to it?

I wish distinctly to say that I do not propose to consider the question of slavery in its moral or religious aspects, but as a political question under the Federal Constitution.

As to my personal opinion in regard to slavery, I am free to say I consider it an evil, which I hope will be eradicated from the earth, but I do not regard it as the greatest of evils, nor do I consider that it requires political action from the Federal government. On the contrary, I believe that while the question of slavery might be safely agitated, with a view to political action, in a consolidated or imperial government, or even in an American Federal State, it cannot under our Federal system of government be safely or rightly agitated as a national question. Its agitation as such has done more to alienate and embitter the two sections of our Union—more to rouse the spirit of slavery aggression and extension, and to tighten the bonds and increase the burdens of the slave, than it has done to effect emancipation. Slavery is an evil permitted by Providence for ends that time will reveal. From this form of social evil, he is still educing good, far more good to the slaves, as a class, than to the masters as a class. It must not be suddenly nor rashly dealt with. Like a disease that pervades the blood or the whole constitution of a man, it needs not, for it cannot be reached by, the exterminating knife or cautery of the surgeon; it requires the gradual, purifying and alterative influences of gentle medicines, that work their way almost imperceptibly to the very principle and seat of the malady.

For my part, while I yield to no man in my love of liberty and the rights of man, I frankly say I had rather that the "rivulet of African slavery" flow on for five hundred years to come, than to see around me the fragments of a dissevered

Union. In that Union, and the silent steady workings of its glorious principles, more than in the conflict of[Pg 15] antagonist and angry parties, rest the hopes, not alone of African emancipation, but of unborn nations.

The American Union grew out of the exigencies of the times. A common cause and a common danger united the colonies first in resistance to the aggressions and exactions of the British government, and finally in the overthrow of its power over them. With the declaration of their independence, came the conviction of the necessity of their permanent Union, and this conviction after much of doubt and debate, resulted in the adoption of the Articles of Confederation by the final ratification of Maryland, on 1st March, 1781, which continued in force until the present Constitution went into operation.

So long as the States were engaged in the war of the Revolution, although the confederation was found to be in many things weak and imperfect, amid the dangers and anxieties of those years of trial its defects were overlooked or supplied by the earnest patriotism of our fathers, and it accomplished its end in the triumph of independence. But it was not long after the peace of 1783, when the Congress came to carry on the Federal government with reference to the ends of peace and the commercial policy and general prosperity of the United States, that it was found that the Articles of Confederation could no longer answer as the Constitution of the United States. A leading writer of that day in addressing the public upon the subject, after enumerating many of the defects of the Confederation with reference to the powers of the Congress, summed up the whole in these brief words, "In short, they may declare everything but do nothing."

Judge Story remarks in speaking of this period of our history—"That the confederation had at least totally failed as an effectual instrument of government. It stood the shadow of a mighty name."

Judge Marshall on the same subject says—"The confederation was apparently expiring from mere debility."

Judge Story further says—"*It is, indeed, difficult to overcharge any picture of the gloom end apprehension which pervaded[Pg 16] the public councils, as well as the private meditations of the ablest men of the country.*"

It was under such circumstances that the convention for forming the present Constitution of the Union was called.

Into this convention were brought by the delegates of the States, the same unceasing jealousy and watchfulness, which had marked the formation of the confederation, in respect to the powers to be confided to the general government.

In the Articles of Confederation it had been declared "that each State retained its sovereignty, freedom and independence, and every power, jurisdiction and right not expressly delegated to the United States."

The States were generally unwilling to surrender anything of their internal sovereignty. They claimed then as they claim now, full right and power to regulate their own domestic institutions in their own way, and were willing to surrender to the general government only such powers as were necessary to the complete efficiency of a Federal government in attaining the purposes of the Union. These were in the language of Alexander Hamilton:

"The common defence of the members; the preservation of the public peace as well against internal convulsions as external attacks; the regulation of commerce with other nations and between the States; the superintendence of our intercourse, political and commercial, with foreign countries."

The difficulty of obtaining a ratification of the Constitution by the people of the States, was not less than the difficulty of framing it in convention. Georgia, New Jersey and Delaware unanimously approved the Constitution. It was supported by large majorities in Pennsylvania, Connecticut, Maryland and South Carolina. It was carried in Massachusetts, New York and Virginia only by a small majority. North Carolina and Rhode Island were the last to adopt it, and the former at first rejected it.

In the address of the convention to Congress on presenting the Constitution with the recommendation for its submission[Pg 17] to and approval by the States, the convention say: "The Constitution which we now present, *is the result of a spirit of amity, and of that mutual deference and concession* which the peculiarity of our political situation rendered indispensable." In these few words of the framers of the Constitution, expressing its reason or spirit, we find the true guide to its interpretation and administration. The spirit of compromise, so far as relates to the clashing views or conflicting interests of different States or sections of the Union, pervades the Constitution in every part, and especially is this the case in reference to the now all-absorbing question of negro slavery.

What was the state of this institution at the adoption of the Constitution, and how did the Constitution deal with it?

The first introduction of African slaves into the American colonies was in 1620. The total number imported by means of the African slave trade between 1715 and 1790, was about 300,000. When the Constitution was ratified in 1790, the total number of slaves in all the States and territories was near 700,000. All the States ratifying the Constitution, except Massachusetts, held slaves; Virginia the largest number—over 293,000; New Hampshire the smallest number—158. Even the granite hills of New Hampshire were not then free from the feet of bondmen.

Our fathers were not responsible for the existence of slavery in their midst. As already stated, the introduction of slaves had commenced in 1620, 156 years before the declaration of independence, and the institution had under the patronage of the British government, insidiously grown up and strengthened itself, especially in the Southern States, which were adapted to negro labor. There it had interwoven itself with the entire fabric of the social and domestic relations, and could not be suddenly or rashly severed without involving greater evils than its own existence.

It is undoubtedly true that a large number of the framers of the Constitution were themselves slaveholders, among them George Washington himself. With these men domestic[Pg 18] slavery, though it might have been regarded as an evil, was certainly not looked upon as a mortal sin, nor were they, whatever might have been their theoretical opinions, practical believers in the doctrine of universal equality of rights or universal suffrage.

Here then, coeval with the organization of the Federal government, was the domestic institution of slavery, existing in all the States but one, and embracing over one sixth of their entire population. There were two very plain methods by which it might have been dealt with. One was by an express declaration of the Constitution, affirming as the Republican sectional party affirm, that slavery is a relic of barbarism, and therefore slavery shall be abolished in all the States and territories of the American Union. Another method was to have declared in the Constitution, as ultra men of the South now declare, that slavery is a benign institution, deserving of protection, encouragement and extension by the Federal government, and therefore slavery shall be protected and extended in all the States and territories of the American Union. Had the constitutional convention been a sectional and not a national organization; had its members been governed by a sectional and not a national spirit, they would doubtless have taken one or the other of the horns of this dilemma, but in that "*spirit of amity, mutual deference and concession,*" which governed their lofty patriotism, they took neither of the extremes. They took the position that the institution of domestic slavery was of local origin and of local concern—a matter directly pertaining to the internal sovereignty of each State; that it was not a legitimate subject for national or Federal legislation, and so far as related to its extension or its abolition within the States, they left it where they found it, with the people of the States whom it most concerned, the Congress assuming only the right, after the period of twenty years, to prohibit the importations of slaves from beyond the limits of the United States. The political reason of this prohibition is apparent. Without it the principle of non-intervention with slavery by the Federal government[Pg 19] which pervades the Constitution, could not have been carried out. So long as the foreign traffic in slaves was made lawful to any of the States, slavery was nationalized. American slave ships, engaged in a lawful commerce, and bearing the national flag, would be as much entitled to national protection as any other of the American mercantile marine. Permission of the African slave trade was essentially intervention in favor of slavery, and the right to prohibit it, and the exercise of that right, in no wise conflict with the principle of non-interference with it within the States.

There are but four provisions of the Constitution wherein the subject of slavery is alluded to, viz: Art. 1, sec. 2; art. 1, sec. 9; art. 4, sec. 2; and art. 5.

It is plain from these provisions—

1st—That the slaveholding States are entitled under the Constitution to representation in the national legislature upon three-fifths of their slaves, so long as slavery exists in those States; and they are subject to direct taxation accordingly.

2d—That the right under State laws to import slaves into *the then existing* States, was guaranteed for twenty years, or until 1808, and the guarded concession of the right involved the converse, that after 1808 the foreign slave trade was to be prohibited by Congress, for the reason already assigned, and any attempt by Congress now to open the African slave trade, would be as direct a moral violation of this compromise of the Constitution as if the Congress were to attempt directly to abolish slavery in any State.

3d—It is equally plain that the right of slave owners to recover fugitive slaves, escaping from the State where they are held, *under the laws thereof,* into another, is guaranteed.

The Federal Constitution so far as relates to the subject of slavery within the United States, involves the three propositions stated and nothing more, and there is nothing in these in the least degree expressing or implying a right in Congress to abolish or establish slavery in any State or territory[Pg 20] of the Union. On the contrary, the whole tenor of the Constitution is, slavery is the creation of *local law*, and Congress is to let it alone.

Now as to the question of slavery in the territories and the power and policy of the Federal government concerning it there.

The power to acquire territory for the purpose of colonization or the creation of States was not expressly granted to the Federal government, either by the Articles of Confederation or by the Constitution, but it has been largely exercised under both systems of government. The acts of the government of the Confederation in accepting cessions from several of the States of unoccupied territory, claimed by them in the west, and organizing territorial governments therein, were declared in 1788, by as high authority as James Madison, to be "*without the least color of constitutional authority.*" But as has been the case with many other usurpations of the Federal and other governments, the value of the ends to be attained seems to have justified the usurpation in the public mind.

The territory acquired by Congress under the Confederation was territory which was claimed by or belonged to certain of the original States. The territory acquired under the Constitution has been foreign territory. Louisiana was acquired in 1803 from France, Florida in 1819 from Spain, Texas in 1846 by annexation as a State, a portion of Oregon in 1846 by a boundary treaty, and a large territory including New Mexico, Utah and California by treaty with Mexico in 1848.

The purchase of Louisiana was a measure of Mr. Jefferson, but so serious were his doubts as to the constitutionality of the purchase, that he advised an amendment of the Constitution, but no such amendment was attempted, and the purchase was finally made and acquiesced in, upon the principle that the end justified the means. It seems now, however, to be generally conceded that the power of the Federal government to acquire territory, exists by implications either in the treaty making power or in the power to[Pg 21] admit new States. In view of the only legitimate end and purpose of all such acquisitions, it is natural to look upon the power of acquiring as an incident of the power to admit new States.

The right or claim of some of the States, viz: New York, Virginia, Massachusetts, Connecticut, North Carolina, South Carolina and Georgia to a vast extent of waste and unoccupied territory, as embraced in their original charters or territorial limits, was a subject of serious concern in the Congress of the Confederation, and constituted for some time the only obstacle to the ratification of the Articles of Confederation. Delaware, Maryland and New Jersey, which had no such territory, were especially jealous on this subject, the two former peremptorily insisting upon the restriction of the boundaries of such of the States as claimed to extend to the Mississippi River or South Sea, to moderate limits, and that the property in the soil of the western territories should be held by the Federal government for the common benefit of all the States, as the same, to use the language of Delaware, "*had been gained by the blood and treasure of all.*"

To remove this subject of contention, New York was the first to tender on 7th March, 1780, a surrender of her claim in western territory. On 6th Sept., 1780, the Congress, by resolution, recommended to the States concerned "a liberal surrender of a portion of their territorial claims, since they cannot be preserved entire without endangering the stability of the general confederacy." On 10th October, 1780, the Congress, by resolution, defined the condition upon which the cession of territory was asked, declaring that "such territory shall be disposed of for the common benefit of the United States, and be settled and formed into distinct republican States, which shall become members of the Federal Union, and have the same rights of sovereignty, freedom and independence as the other States."

Governed by that noble patriotism and devotion to the good of the Union, which marked the whole course of the revolution, and the foundation of the general government,[Pg 22] all the States rose above the dictates of selfishness and State pride, and laid upon the altar of the Union, gifts that have grown to empires. The surrender of territory asked for by New Jersey, Maryland and Delaware, and recommended by Congress, was made. All the States but Georgia had ceded prior to the adoption of the Constitution. The cession of Georgia was completed in 1802. With the immense domain of fair and fertile lands, thus freely given to the Federal government by individual States, it was able to discharge the debts of the war of the revolution, and in various ways to provide for the common defence and promote the general welfare of the United States. No man in whose bosom glows a generous sentiment, can read the record of that period of our national history without feeling his heart swell with admiration and affection for the fathers of the Republic. Would that their sons would ever honor their memory by an imitation of their noble example of devotion to the Union!

In this surrender of territory to the general government, we distinctly mark, and it is for that purpose I have related the history, the same "spirit of amity, and of mutual deference and concession," which pervades the Constitution, and I would dwell here a moment to ask you, and especially sectional Republicans, who think that no good thing can come out of the Nazareth of the South, to note another fact:

that of all the territory ceded to the United States by individual States, for the common benefit of the Union, by far the largest part was owned by what were then and are now Slave States. Massachusetts, New York, and Connecticut claimed largely, but without possessory right. Virginia, North Carolina, South Carolina and Georgia had superior claims to nearly all. The splendid empire that now embraces the States of Ohio, Indiana, Illinois, Michigan, Kentucky and Wisconsin was most of it once the property of the sovereign State of Virginia. Yet Virginia, then the largest slaveholding State of the Union, laid all this vast territory at the feet of the Union, with no other reward than the consciousness of love of[Pg 23] country. She did not even stipulate for the preservation of her own "*peculiar institution.*" Virginia has not alone given to the nation Washington, Jefferson, Madison, Monroe, Harrison, Clay, Henry, Marshall, heroes, statesmen and Presidents, whose valor aided to win our independence, and whose wisdom laid deep and broad the foundations of our Union, but by her magnanimity she added to the Union six of its noblest States, and from their citizens at least she should never hear the cry that taunts her with slavery. Rather let that cry go forth from puritan and abolition Massachusetts, as her sons read over her ancient Quaker laws, or count up the nefarious gains their slave-trading fathers made, while enjoying the twenty years lease of the African slave trade, granted by the Federal Constitution. Ridicule as we may the family pride or State pride of Virginia, or the sometimes Quixotic chivalry of her sons, they have reason to be proud of their noble mother, for her great names belong to American fame, and her history is our nation's glory. In view of all the past, I hope that day may never come when Virginia shall cease to be one of the Union as our fathers made it.

Over the territory thus acquired, the Congress of the Confederation had adopted two systems of government; viz:

the ordinance of April 23, 1784, prepared by Thomas Jefferson, soon superseded by the more celebrated ordinance of July 13, 1787, prepared by Nathan Dane of Massachusetts. In its extent the first ordinance covered *all territory* ceded or to be ceded; the second ordinance covered only the territory north west of the Ohio.

I shall not refer to the Jefferson ordinance of 1784, further than to note these points concerning it.

First—It provided for temporary government, by which the people of the territory might regulate their own internal affairs free from the control of Congress; and,

Second—It did not prohibit slavery—a provision for that purpose having been stricken out by the vote of Southern States. This ordinance was superseded, as before stated, by that of July 13, 1787.[Pg 24]

On the terms of this ordinance and its subsequent recognition under the Constitution, rests much of the argument of the advocates of Congressional intervention to prohibit slavery in the territories. This ordinance, as you doubtless all know, forever prohibited slavery in all the North west territory, but contained also the proviso for the surrender of fugitive slaves. I ask you to note in regard to the ordinance.

First—It applied only to territory acquired from Virginia north of the Ohio, and it was unanimously adopted; and it was a sufficient legal and moral ground for its recognition by the Congress after the adoption of the Federal Constitution, that the ordinance, whether made with or without authority, was in its terms a compact between *all the States*, and was recognized by all the States as such by tacit assent, if not express legislation. It was expressly so recognized by Virginia, Georgia and North Carolina.

Consent had cured the usurpation of the Congress, if such it was, as Madison affirmed, and therefore, the ordinance, when the Constitution took effect, was legally and constitutionally *an engagement of the United States, under the Confederation*, binding upon the Federal government by express provision of the sixth article of the Constitution, declaring that "all debts contracted and engagements entered into before the adoption of this Constitution, shall be as valid against the United States under this Constitution, as under the Confederation." It was upon this legal ground, as well as upon the ground that Indiana was not adapted to and did not need slave labor, that Congress refused to allow the petitions of Indiana while a territory, which petitions were approved by William Henry Harrison, for a suspension for a term of years of the sixth article of the ordinance of 1787, prohibiting slavery. It was a compact to which all the States were parties, and by its express terms, could not be repealed or suspended without their common consent.

Second—The prohibition of the ordinance, applied to territory substantially free from slavery, and which it was[Pg 25] well understood was not adapted to slave labor. It raised no such question, as would have been raised, if it had been applied to territory where slavery then largely existed, or which was adapted to negro slave labor. It is, therefore, no precedent for Congressional action in such a case. The precedent of one case is not a rule of decision for another, unless the two are substantially alike. This noble ordinance of 1787, then rather affirmed a principle of freedom, than imposed a necessary practical prohibition, for it may be well to know, that notwithstanding the ordinance, there were as late as 1810, in Indiana, 237 slaves, and as late as 1820, in Illinois, 917 slaves, but upon a soil fitted by nature for the vigorous growth of freedom, African slavery, the tree of tropic climes, could not grow, and it withered and died, as it had done before in New Hampshire, Vermont,

Massachusetts, Connecticut, Rhode Island, New York, New Jersey and Pennsylvania.

In connexion with the ordinance of 1787, another point may be alluded to here. In a very able speech made by Mr. Upham of Massachusetts, in opposition to the Kansas and Nebraska bill in the House of Representatives on 10th of May 1854, the point is made, that the prohibition of slavery in the ordinance of 1787, and the provisions of the Constitution regarding slavery, were the result of a bargain between the North and the South, by which the North gained on one hand exclusion of slavery from the North-west territory, and the right first to tax, and after twenty years to prohibit the African slave trade, and the South on the other hand gained the right to representation in slaves, the right to continue to import them for twenty years, and the right forever to reclaim fugitive slaves. According to this theory, the slave representation, the reclamation of fugitive slaves, and the right to twenty years of the African slave trade, were, to use Mr. Upham's language "the equivalent paid by the free States to the Slave States, in consideration of the abandonment by the Slave States of all claim to extend their slavery beyond their own limits." It is undoubtedly true, that the ordinance of 1787 and the[Pg 26] Constitution were almost concurrent acts, but the facts of history will not sustain Mr. Upham's assumption of a bargain to the extent stated, yet it has sufficient basis to warrant the point, that the ordinance of 1787 was a compact and a compromise, and was never intended by the South as a concession of any right or power in Congress arbitrarily to prohibit slavery in any territory of the United States. It may be true that for their consent to have slavery excluded from the North-west territory, the South received an equivalent, but the exclusion and the equivalent applied only to the North west territory, and as to all territory thereafter acquired, the question remained the same as before the ordinance of 1787, and must depend on the

Constitution itself, unaffected by the precedent of the ordinance. Let us consider the question under the Constitution.

It was resolved at the Republican Convention of 1856 in Philadelphia, and I do not understand the Republican party of 1860 to have abandoned the position, "That the Constitution of the United States confers upon Congress sovereign power over the territories of the United States for their government, and that in the exercise of this power, it is both *the right* and *the duty* of Congress *to prohibit* in the territories, those twin relics of barbarism, polygamy and slavery."

This sweeping assertion of sovereign power in Congress over citizens of the United States in territories, of course affirms that Congress can do for the territories all or even more than a State government can do for a State. Mr. John Pettit, late United States Senator from Indiana, has made the broadest assertion of Congressional sovereignty, for he has said and endeavored to prove that it is *"absolute, unconditional, unlimited authority"*; such, in fact, as would enable the Federal government to sell the citizens of the territories into slavery. Power to do an act is one thing—a constitutional right to do it is another. I do not concede Mr. Pettit's authority for Congressional sovereignty, even though he be one of Mr. Buchanan's Judges in Nebraska, but it is interesting to note, by way of parenthesis, how[Pg 27] wonderfully Republican doctrine on one extreme, and Buchanan or Breckinridge doctrine on the other, work together to a common center, Congressional or Federal government despotism.

It is vain to look for any express warrant for any such power in the Constitution, except in the language of the 3d section of the 4th article, declaring that—"*The Congress shall have power to dispose of and make all needful rules and regulations respecting the territory or other property of the United States."*

Assuming that this is a grant of power to govern the people of United States territory, in the ordinary sense of sovereign legislative power, such as that possessed by the States for example, this anomalous conclusion would follow: that there are under the Constitution two distinct systems of government—one a strictly defined and limited Federal government over the States, with a right of representation in the governed; another a municipal government, almost arbitrary in its character over the citizens in the territories as mere colonists, without any right of representation in the governed. There is no foundation for this conclusion. When the Constitution was adopted, the territories were recognized as incipient or inchoate States. It was with reference to them that the power to admit new States was incorporated in the Constitution. People migrating to those territories carried with them the inherent rights of self-government and the guarantees of the Constitution. The Constitution was intended for the territories as much as for the States that made it. Congress has no power but what it derives from the Constitution. If it can acquire territory and govern it, it can do so only by virtue of and in accordance with the Constitution. We cannot suppose that the framers of the Constitution, or the people of the States who spoke through it, looking as many of them did, to the fair lands of the west, as their own future homes and the homes of brothers and children, where fortunes broken in the revolutionary struggle might be retrieved, would impose on themselves or those brothers and[Pg 28] children a colonial bondage to the Federal government, worse than that from which they had just escaped. Jealousy of the power of the Federal government, as already shown, had been the great drawback to the confederacy and to the formation of the Constitution, and had carefully guarded in the Constitution the rights of the States as to all matters of internal sovereignty, and it must be so construed as equally to guard the rights of the people of the territories or inchoate States, or the Constitution becomes incongruous and inconsistent. Power of exclusive legislation was conferred on Congress, as to certain defined localities acquired for specific purposes, such as a seat of government, arsenals, &c., all other powers of legislation were Federal, not municipal—powers to govern the States or their people for national or Federal purposes, not powers to govern the people in the States for internal or domestic purposes. This reasonable view of the Constitution forces the conclusion that we must regard the power to make rules and regulations as to the territory and other property of the United States, as relating solely to the protection and disposal of the public territory as land or property, and we must therefore find the power to govern the territories involved or implied, as it doubtless is in the power to admit new States. The end of acquiring territory is the formation of States, and the powers of territorial government, so far as power was conferred upon Congress, must have had reference to that end. Therefore it is, that the duty and the function of Congress are alike filled in the civil government of a territory, when the Congress shall have defined a mode or an organization by which the citizens in a territory shall be able to exercise their inherent right of self-government in accordance with the principles of the Constitution. No man pretends that Congress has any power of legislation over the internal or domestic affairs of a sovereign State. All matters of internal sovereignty are left to the people of such State, and there is no reason to be found in the Constitution or in the nature of the case, why Congress should have any greater power over the internal[Pg 29] or domestic concerns of citizens in a territory than it has over those of citizens in a State. It is not true that the territories are outside of the Constitution, and become entitled to it and its sacred bill of rights by grace of an act of Congress. That is, indeed, strange doctrine to apply to an American citizen standing on his own territorial soil, which Congress had no right to acquire or govern at all, except by virtue of the Constitution, and it assumes too much, for this reason: All power not granted to Congress is reserved to the States or the people; and if the territories are not under the Constitution, there is no right in Congress to govern them at all, and that right rests in the States or the people who settle the territories. On the contrary, if the territories be under the Constitution, then must they be governed according to its principles and bill of rights, and not arbitrarily, and all powers of government over them not granted to Congress are in the people of the territories themselves. Powers of municipal legislation as to internal affairs, as already stated, are not granted, therefore are they in the people. If this doctrine of arbitrary Congressional sovereignty be correct, then have citizens in the territories no constitutional rights, and no franchise except at Congressional discretion—they may be put and kept under martial law as long as Congress pleases, and this without respect to population—they may be sold into slavery according to John Pettit—and this system of military provincial government may be kept up so long as the Federal government can control an army to carry it out. Does any man believe there is any constitutional right in Congress to do any such thing? The statement of the proposition is its best refutation. How much more logical and consistent then, is it to refer the powers of Congress to legislate for the territories, to the end of all legislation either for acquiring or governing territory, viz: the formation of States, equal in sovereignty on all questions to the original States. If then, the question of domestic slavery be a local question to be decided by the people of the States as they see fit, and such the whole theory of the[Pg 30] Constitution assumes it to be, it is equally a local question to be decided by the people of the territories as they see fit. If the people of a territory when they come to form a State Constitution, are competent and have the right to decide the slavery question for themselves, as all concede to be the case, then there is no argument consistent with the principle on which our institutions are based, of any avail to show, that the same territorial people have not equal right and capacity under a territorial government, and before they form a State Constitution, to decide the question of slavery for themselves by local legislation. If the people of a territory are competent to make a Constitution without the assent of Congress, for a stronger reason they are competent to make a law below the dignity of a Constitution. It will not do for any man to contend that mere change of residence from a State to a territory, so changes the moral and intellectual character of the man, as to unfit him for the exercise of self-government, or the high duties of founder of a State. The experience of the nation disproves this position. Some of the strongest and best minds known to American history have grown up on the frontier and among the hardships of border life. High mental cultivation or the refinements and elegancies of social life are not necessary to the founders of States. Heroic and manly virtues, and intellectual powers, are often developed amid the trials which beset the emigrant and the pioneer. Like the oak which takes deeper root from the rockings of the storm, true manhood enlarges and strengthens itself by the conflict with adversity and privation. History records the obligations Ohio and Kentucky owe to Daniel Boone and Simon Kenton. Beneath the leathern hunting shirts of those bold pioneers beat the hearts of heroes. They were types of many squatter sovereigns known to history, and of many more

"Illustrious masters of a name unknown."

In the territory of Indiana, William Henry Harrison and Zachary Taylor, two of the Presidents of the United States, laid in early manhood the basis of character that has made[Pg

31] them famous. If you would know of what material squatter sovereigns are made, look over the territorial history of the North-west. Look to the early history of Ohio, Indiana and Illinois. Of one of these squatter sovereigns, Manasseh Cutler, of Hamilton, Massachusetts, it has been said, "Beneath the shelter of the covered wagon in which he started from his village home in Massachusetts to found Marietta, the imperial State of Ohio was wrapped up. He was truly a philosopher and a patriarch. He was more than a statesman—he was the founder of a State."

What says Judge Burnett, of Cincinnati, himself a squatter sovereign, of the first territorial legislature of the North-west territory? He says:

"In choosing members to the first Territorial Legislature, the people in almost every instance, selected their strongest and best men in their respective counties. Party influence was scarcely felt; and it may be said with confidence, that no legislature has been chosen under the State government which contained a larger proportion of aged, intelligent men, than were found in that body. Many of them, it is true, were unacquainted with the forms and practical duties of legislation; but they were strong-minded, sensible men, acquainted with the condition and wants of the country, and could form correct opinions of the operation of any measure proposed for their consideration." He further adds, "several members of that assembly were men of the first order of talents; and, with scarcely an exception, they would all be now estimated as well qualified for State legislation." Away then with the idea that there are not in the manly form, the courageous and generous heart, the clear and self-reliant, though, perhaps, untutored mind of the pioneer of the forest and prairie, "native countryman," though he may be, equally with "the exile from foreign lands," or the residents of towns and cities, the inherent right of self-government, and the elements that lay broad and deep the foundations of free and sovereign States! As for me, I had rather trust the interests of American liberty and the destiny of American institutions to the keeping of[Pg 32] the men, who in the encounter of hardships that make men heroes, have opened in the wilderness the pathway of civilization, and made its waste places to blossom like the rose, than to trust these priceless treasures to the keeping of many of the merchant princes of our eastern cities, whose warehouses and whose homes are palaces, "whose ledger is their Bible and whose gold is their God"; or to the still worse keeping of such Federal administrations as that of James Buchanan—a man in whose veins, according to his own boast, never flowed a drop of democratic blood.

It is not to such men I would commit the welfare of the territories of the United States. Rather let freeborn white men govern them *in their own way*, unawed by Federal armies sustaining Lecompton Constitutions, and I have no fear of the domestic institutions that will be formed in the territories, nor any fears for the Union and the Constitution.

To sum up what I have said on this part of my argument, the proposition is simply this: The Constitution, considered as a whole, and interpreted as it should be, as the act of a moral person, made for great moral and political ends, and not by the mere technical rules which lawyers or impracticable theorists would apply to it, requires that the people of a territory or inchoate State of the United States, preparatory to their admission to the rank of a full grown State within the Union, shall have as full power, through a legislature of their own choosing, to deal with the subject of domestic slavery, and with other subjects of domestic concern, as is possessed by the people of States in the Union. In other words, I say, that whatever may be the right and duty of Congress under the Constitution to guard and protect the territories from

internal or foreign violence, and to maintain their allegiance
to the Union, it is neither the right nor duty of Congress,
under the Constitution, to interfere with the question of
slavery or any other domestic question, so long as the people
of the territories are faithful to their allegiance to the
Constitution and the Federal Republic.

I now proceed to state and confirm by brief historic
evidence[Pg 33] a proposition already implied in what I have
said upon the compromise character of the Constitution and
the ordinance of 1787. It is this: The action of the Federal
government on the subject of slavery has been essentially
compromise action. It recognizes the principle of the co-
existence and extension of Free States and Slave States,
under and within the confederacy, leaving the ultimate of the
question of abolition or extension, not with the Congress, but
with the people of the several States. Congress has never
rightfully taken sides on this question; for while on the one
hand slavery has been forbidden in some territories, it has
been permitted in others. Slave territory and free territory
have alike been acquired by treaty, and Slave States and Free
States alike admitted to the Union. The action of Congress is
therefore no precedent for absolute slavery prohibition or
indefinite slavery extension. Having never been exercised
but by way of compromise it commits the government to
neither extreme and is not a conclusive precedent for the
constitutional power of Congress over the subject.

I shall briefly notice the facts of history bearing on this
proposition.

The territory now covered by the States of Tennessee,
Alabama, and Mississippi, was ceded to the United States by
North Carolina and Georgia prior to 1803, and accepted by
the United States, on the condition that Congress should
extend over it a government, and ultimately divide it into

States, on the principles of the ordinance of 1787, *except as to slavery*, and territorial governments were afterwards organized over it as slave territory. While, therefore, Congress had in 1787 assumed, by a compact of the original States, to prohibit slavery north-west of the Ohio River, it had also within twelve years after the adoption of the ordinance of 1787 and the Constitution, by express contract agreed not to prohibit it in all territory south of the Ohio, and by the admission of Kentucky and Tennessee as Slave States prior to 1800, could not prohibit it there.[Pg 34]

Up then to the time of the purchase of Louisiana in 1803, the Ohio River was the compromise line between free and slave territory—*a line of agreement*, rather than arbitrary legislation.

Louisiana was all slave territory, and by the 3d article of the treaty for its acquisition, its inhabitants were to come into the Union as soon as possible on equal terms with other citizens, and in the meantime their rights of religion, liberty and property were to be maintained and protected.

In this territory, the boundaries of which were subsequently defined by treaties with Spain and Great Britain, were included the present States of Louisiana, Arkansas, Missouri, Iowa, Minnesota, Oregon, and the territories of Kansas, Nebraska, &c.

Soon after this acquisition, territorial governments were organized over the southern portion of the territory, without prohibition of slavery. In 1812, Louisiana was admitted as a Slave State, and Arkansas and Missouri were subsequently organized as territories without prohibition of slavery.

In 1819, Florida was acquired by treaty with Spain, with the same stipulation, as in the treaty in regard to Louisiana, that the inhabitants were to have the rights and privileges of citizens of the United States and be admitted into the Union; and soon after the territory of Florida was organized without prohibition of slavery.

From 1787 until the Missouri question came up, no successful attempt was made by Congress to prohibit slavery in any territory of the United States. In 1817, Missouri applied for admission to the Union. Her admission as a Slave State was strenuously contested, and to the act authorizing her to form a State Constitution was appended a provision applying the 6th or anti-slavery section of the ordinance of 1787 to all the territory ceded by Louisiana, outside of the limits of Missouri, and north of 36 deg. 30 min. north latitude, or the southern boundary of Missouri. The adoption of this act, fixing a geographical line between[Pg 35] Free States and Slave States, has been called a compromise. The proposition was beyond doubt made in the spirit of compromise, and received the support of compromise men, but the North who insisted upon the exclusion of Missouri with a slave constitution, generally voted against the act in its final passage, and the South, for the sake of getting Missouri in with a slave constitution, as generally voted for it. The compromise was not acceptable to either side, and when Missouri presented her Constitution in 1821 for the approval of Congress, her admission was again opposed by Northern men, and made conditional upon her declaration by solemn act of her legislature, that a clause of her Constitution relating to free negroes and mulattoes, should not be construed to authorize any law violating the privileges and immunities of any citizen of either of the States of the Union, under the Constitution of the United States. Missouri made the declaration required, and by proclamation of the President, became a State on August 10th, 1821. The resolution of Congress of 2d March, 1821, was beyond doubt the real condition or compromise upon which Missouri was admitted, and it was in this compromise and not in that of 1820, that Henry Clay took part. Strange as it may seem; it is nevertheless true, that notwithstanding the alleged compromise of 1820, an attempt was made in 1821 by Northern men in Congress to override that compromise,— that "sacred compact," that "plighted faith," that "landmark of freedom,"—and to keep Missouri out of the Union, because she had adopted in her Constitution a provision to prevent free negroes or mulattoes from coming to or settling in the State—a provision which is contained in the present Constitutions of Indiana and Illinois, and has been enforced in Constitutions or legislation of other Northern States, and was sanctioned by the people of Indiana in 1851, when submitted to them as a distinct proposition, by a vote of 100,976 for it, to 21,066 against it. By that vote, Indiana as late as 1851 affirmed that Missouri was right and Congress wrong in the great conflict of 1821.[Pg 36]

The high and sacred character of a national compact has been claimed for the Missouri act of 6th March, 1820. No man who will calmly and intelligently and without prejudice examine its history, can fail to see that however expedient it might have been at the time, there is no compact—no sacred character about it. Looking on the whole question as one of constitutional power and policy, I am free to say I think the South and not the North were in the right in the Missouri controversy.

What are the plain facts? In 1803 the territory embracing Missouri had been acquired as slave territory. It had been organized by Congress in 1804 as slave territory. The inhabitants under the foreign and territorial law had acquired and held slaves, as rightfully as they were held in any State. No prohibition of slavery had been extended over the territory. By the treaty with France and the settled policy of the Federal government, the territory of Missouri, when it had attained a sufficient population, was entitled to admission as a State on an equal footing with the original States. In 1817 Missouri asked of Congress authority to form a State Constitution, preparatory to her admission to the Union. Her case was in all its cardinal and essential features precisely parallel to that of Kentucky, Tennessee, Mississippi and Louisiana, which had already been admitted as Slave States without question, and how was she met? Northern men in Congress, in effect said to her, if you choose to come into the Union as a Free State, we will let you in; if not, we will keep you out, and under our arbitrary power of government, until you get rid of your slaves. We don't believe in slavery, and don't mean to have any more barbarian slaveholders in our company. Northern men in Congress, in violation of the spirit and policy of the Constitution, which recognized slavery as a purely local institution, endeavored to compel a full grown sovereign State to abolish slavery. That is the whole point of the case. It is not surprising that this position and attempt of the North should have awakened a spirit of resistance in the South that shook the[Pg 37] Union to its very center. Whatever might be the opinion of Northern men as to the power of Congress over slavery in the territories, or as to the expediency of prohibiting it, it was too late to apply their doctrine to Missouri. She was ripe for admission to the Union as a State, with domestic institutions formed to suit her people, and formed, too, under the eye and sanction of Congress, and Congress had no right to make her State sovereignty dependent on the carrying out *as to other territory*, of the Northern idea of prohibiting slavery. The case of Missouri should have been decided on its own merits.

In view of all the facts, and of its proposed restraint upon the constitutional power of new States besides Missouri, I fully believe the Supreme Court of the United States correctly laid down the law in the Dred Scott decision, declaring the 8th section of the act of 6th March, 1820, being the prohibition of slavery, to be unconstitutional and void, for the simple reason that it was the right *of the people* of those new States to make a constitution or laws for or against slavery as they saw fit, and not the right of the Congress, which has no power under its own Constitution to make State Constitutions.

The principle of compromise embraced in the Missouri line, whether legal or not, calmed the agitation of the question of slavery, which had, during the Missouri struggle, assumed a dangerous form. It shut out slavery in the vast region north of 36 deg. 30 min., not adapted to slave labor, and permitted it south of that line where slavery had taken or was likely to take root. Therefore when Arkansas applied in 1836 for admission as a Slave State, she came in without serious controversy, though northern opposition in Congress was not even then silent.

Between the establishment of Texan independence in 1836 and her annexation to the United States in 1845, in view of the latter event, the question of slavery extension became one of absorbing interest to the nation. The Democratic party recognized it in the 7th article of their platform in their National Convention of 1840, taking the[Pg 38] true ground of non-intervention by Congress. In 1843 the Liberty party, so called, organized upon the distinct ground of opposition to slavery. In 1844 the Democratic party reaffirmed their platform of 1840, and declared in favor of annexing Texas, and its candidates were sustained by the people. In 1845 the Congressional agitation was resumed on the question of annexing Texas. It resulted in the annexation, upon the compromise of extending the Missouri compromise line of 36 deg. 30 min. across the Texan territory, leaving a disputed boundary north of that line, which was adjusted in 1850 by making 36 deg. 30 min. the north boundary of Texas.

In 1846 the question of prohibition again came up in Congress on the bill to organize a territorial government for Oregon, and was kept in agitation until Oregon was forced, for self-protection to form a provisional government; and after a proposition of Mr. Douglas, sustained by the Senate, to extend the Missouri compromise line to the Pacific, had been voted down in the House by northern votes, the Oregon bill was finally passed in 1848, with the proviso of the ordinance of 1787 against slavery, the South voting in a body against its passage—not because they expected slavery to go there, but because they wanted the Missouri line of compromise extended to the Pacific.

In 1846 and 1847 the slavery agitation raged fiercely in the nation and in Congress upon the question of applying a slavery prohibition in the form known as the Wilmot proviso to all the territory to be acquired from Mexico under the treaty, the negotiations for which were then pending. The Wilmot proviso was voted down, and the treaty was consummated Feb. 2, 1848, and Mexican territory, embracing California, Utah and New Mexico was acquired without prohibition of slavery, but the territory was free under the Mexican law, and all Mexican inhabitants who should elect to become citizens of the United States, were entitled to become so at the proper time to be judged of by Congress, and to be incorporated into the Federal Union according to the principles of the Constitution.[Pg 39]

At the commencement of the session of the XXXIst Congress in 1849, the slavery agitation had reached a degree of intensity before unknown. The territory acquired from Mexico, in consequence of this agitation had been left without civil government. California, full of northern emigrants in search of gold, had in the absence of any action of Congress, exercised her inherent right of self-government and formed a State Constitution prohibiting slavery, and was asking admission to the Union. Utah and New Mexico were ripe for territorial governments. The Texan boundary was unsettled. The South was opposing the admission of California as a Free State and insisting on its division, and demanding the distinct legalization of slavery in the territories south of the Missouri line of 36 deg. 30 min., and the extension of that line to the Pacific, and demanding also a more stringent fugitive slave law, and the North was demanding the admission of California and the establishment of the Wilmot proviso over all the territory to be organized, and demanding also the immediate abolition of slavery in the District of Columbia.

The contest for speaker in the House continued from the 3d to the 22d December, 1849, resulting in the election of Howell Cobb over R. C. Winthrop. So ominous of trouble were the signs of the political sky, that President Taylor, in his annual message, took occasion to caution the Congress against the introduction of topics of a sectional character, and to repeat the solemn warning of Washington against furnishing any ground for characterizing parties by geographical discriminations.

The history of the legislation of 1850 is too well known to need detail here. It resulted in another compromise, by which six important measures all involving the slavery question were adopted. These were

1. The admission of California as a free State.

2. The settlement of the Texas boundary, limiting its northern line to 36 deg. 30 min.

3. The formation of territorial government for Utah, and

4. The like for New Mexico.[Pg 40]

5. The abolition of the slave trade in the District of Columbia, and

6. The Fugitive slave law.

California, Utah, New Mexico and Texas all embraced territory on both sides of the Missouri Compromise line. California was the first State south of that line that had ever asked for admission to the Union with a Constitution excluding slavery.

The cardinal feature of the Compromise of 1850 was the abandonment of a geographical line to separate free and slave territory, and the distinct recognition of the principle of non-intervention by Congress with slavery. The compromise in terms recognized the right of the people of the territories to be admitted to the Union with or without slavery as they might desire—that was its very essence as distinguished from the Compromise of 1820.

The principle of non-intervention in the territories had been logically involved, in the national platforms of the democratic party since 1840, but it had never until 1850 received the direct sanction of the Congress.

The legislation of 1850 must be regarded as one of the most memorable events in our constitutional and political history. It received the aid and sanction of some of the ablest and wisest statesmen the nation has ever known.—There were men in the Senate taking part in the controversy that resulted in the compromise, whose political lives had commenced when the fathers of the Republic were ruling its affairs. Clay, Benton, Webster and Calhoun were there, and the South and the North alike were represented by their ablest men. It had become their high duty to settle by an enduring principle the future policy of the nation as to the organization of territorial government for the national domain, and as to the admission of new States. The antagonisms of the North and South, fostered on the one hand by the spirit of abolition, and on the other by the spirit of slavery extension; and still more fostered by the long continued and unconstitutional attempts of Congress to deal with the question, by splitting the difference[Pg 41] between the contending sections, could no longer be reconciled by a boundary line. With every fresh acquisition of national territory, the zeal of the contending power overleaped the congressional boundary, and demanded more for its own sectional policy.

In the Congress of 1850 the Northern or Free soil party insisted on the absolute prohibition of slavery in all the new territory acquired from Mexico. They were able as they had been before when Mr. Douglas proposed, and the South voted for it, to vote down the project of extending the Missouri Compromise line to the Pacific. The South with such Northern men as were opposed to the Wilmot proviso, were able to defeat that. Neither the Missouri Compromise nor the Wilmot proviso could be carried.—The "irrepressible conflict," long encouraged by selfish political schemers or over-zealous, if not fanatical theorists, had reached a crisis, and the nation looked on in fear.

Then it was that the great and patriotic men who carried the compromise of 1850, said to the South and to the North, we will henceforth make no line over the national domain to mark out the boundary between Free States and Slave States. Before the law of the Constitution, both Free States and Slave States are equal. The territory of which we are the trustees belongs neither to Northern institutions, nor to Southern institutions. We will not interfere, for we have no right to interfere, to give it exclusively to either. It is now free territory by the Mexican law. We will not extend slavery over it, nor will we exclude slavery from it; but we open the territory to citizens of all the States alike. It is their common property. The land is all before them where to choose; let them go in with their wives and their children, their men servants and their maid servants, their goods and their cattle, and the stranger that is within their gates, and form such domestic institutions as may suit their wants and desires, consistent with republican government and the Federal Constitution, which is for them, as for us, the supreme law. Let *the people*, who are to constitute States in all that wide domain, decide for[Pg 42] themselves, for they will best know, what fundamental or temporary laws they want, and the Federal government will protect them in their free choice. When they come to us matured, as California now is, into republican States, we will admit them to our common Union on an equal footing with the original States in all respects whatsoever, "with or without slavery, as their Constitution may prescribe at the time of their admission."

Here at last was found the true solution of the question of slavery in its relations to the Federal government, and it was adopted by the Congress and accepted by the nation; for both the Democratic and Whig parties, then the great dividing political parties, united upon it as common ground in the presidential canvass of 1852. One party, however, styling itself the *Free Soil Democracy*, the remnant of the party that had in 1848 supported Martin Van Buren for the presidency upon the Buffalo platform of "*no more Slave States—no more Slave Territory*," did meet in convention, at Pittsburgh, on 11th August, 1852, to denounce in no measured language the compromise of 1850 and slavery in general. I notice this party now only to refer you at your leisure to its platform, and to ask you to note that the President of the Convention was Henry Wilson of Massachusetts, and its nominees for President and Vice-President were John P. Hale of New Hampshire, and George W. Julian of Indiana. Two of these gentlemen are now Republican Senators in Congress, and the third, Mr. Julian, a member elect from Indiana to the House of Representatives in Congress. These gentlemen were known in 1852 as *Free Soil Abolitionists*, in 1860 they are known by the more fashionable and pleasant-sounding name of Republicans.

The principle of non-intervention, on which the compromise of 1850 was based, was in itself so simple, so just, so consistent with the Constitution and the democratic theory of our institutions, that it could not but prevail. Out of 3,143,679 votes cast for President in 1852, Mr. Hale received 155,825, leaving 2,987,854 as the popular vote in favor of the compromise of 1850.[Pg 43]

I rejoice to know that in that great struggle to establish sound and enduring constitutional principle, to rule the Federal government on the question of slavery, the Whig party and its noble old leaders, were as they had ever been, on the side of the Union and the Constitution. The compromise of 1850 was with Webster and Clay the crowning achievement of illustrious lives, and having accomplished this great work, they soon—

"Sustained and soothed by an unfaltering trust,
Drew around them the drapery of the couch of death,
And laid down to pleasant dreams,"

full of years and full of honors.

The compromise of 1850 touched the true principle of dealing with slavery, but it was not a perfect work. It left upon the statute book of the nation, legislation still operating over United States territory, directly opposed to the principle of non-intervention, which the nation had almost unanimously approved. The principle of the compromise of 1850, and the principle of permission or prohibition involved in a geographical line to divide Free and Slave States, were directly inconsistent with each other, and sooner or later this inconsistency had to be met and removed. For the Congress to say, as they did in the compromise of 1850, that the people of Texas, Utah and New Mexico, should be admitted to the Union as Free States or as Slave States, as they might choose, and at the same time to affirm as they did by retaining, or at least not formally erasing, the Missouri compromise line and the Oregon prohibition, that the people of Kansas, Nebraska and Oregon, and all the north-west territories should come into the Union as Free States or not at all, was a glaring inconsistency, and discrimination, not in favor of the North, but in favor of the South. Men in Oregon wanting domestic slaves could not have them. Men in Utah and New Mexico wanting slaves could have them or not, as they pleased. One man in the nation was found able enough, and brave enough, and patriotic enough to grapple with this question and bring it to the test, and carry out to its logical results the doctrine of the compromise of 1850; and[Pg 44] that he bore himself bravely and well through the trying ordeal, and against fearful odds, even his bitterest foes must admit.

Stephen A. Douglas, of Illinois, was but 37 years of age when he stood in the United States Senate, one of the ablest of the supporters of the compromise of 1850. His own hand had drawn the bills to admit California as a Free State, and to organize Utah and New Mexico. Among the venerable princes of the Senate, he was their equal, and Henry Clay, the noblest Roman of them all, moved by Mr. Douglas' magnanimity on that occasion, pronounced him to be "the most generous man living."

In 1854 Mr. Douglas carried through the Congress of the United States and through a parliamentary warfare, in which no other man than he could have triumphed, the bill to organize the territories of Kansas and Nebraska, declaring inoperative and void the Missouri geographical compromise line, and affirming the true intent and meaning of the Kansas and Nebraska act to be, "*to leave the people of any State or territory perfectly free to form and regulate their domestic institutions in their own way, subject only to the Constitution of the United States.*"

In this short "*stump speech in the belly of the bill,*" as Thomas H. Benton and Republican orators after him have, by way of ridicule, been pleased to call it, is the key to the law which must ever govern its true interpretation, and it puts to the rout all the arguments that have been made to prove that non-intervention and popular or territorial sovereignty are not in the Kansas and Nebraska bill, except in small fractions.

A measure so radical and far-reaching as the formal annulling of the Missouri compromise line, could not fail to meet at first with terrific opposition. It broke in on old habits and ways of thinking—it stirred up men's opinions to the roots—it took thought from the surface and forms of things to their substance—it brought democracy to the test. It put to the nation the pregnant questions: Are the rights of white men and black men, the claims of freedom and humanity[Pg 45] to be trusted to the white men of the American territories, as well as American States, or are they not? Are free white American citizens in American territories, as well as American States, competent to decide the question of African slavery or not? Are they competent to govern themselves or not? It did more than this; it laid the ax of Anglo-Saxon democracy at the root of the tree of African slavery.

No man was more sincerely opposed to the annulling of the Missouri compromise line than myself; but I am free to say, that with my prejudices in favor of freedom and Free States, and the reputed sacredness of the Missouri line, I did not look on both sides of the question. I condemned Mr. Douglas and I condemned him unheard. I have endeavored to retrieve that error by a more thorough examination, and I am now convinced that he was in the right and his opponents were in the wrong, and to that conviction will the nation come at last.

The defeat of Fremont and the condemnation of the Republican or Philadelphia platform of 1856 by a majority upon the popular vote of 1,371,430 votes, was an unequivocal endorsement by the people, not only of the compromise of 1850, but of the Kansas and Nebraska bill in its erasure of the Missouri line. Had James Buchanan been a wise statesman and a patriot, as I fear he is not; had he carried in his veins "a single drop of democratic blood," Kansas under the operation of the principle of non-intervention by Congress, and intervention by its own people with the question of slavery, would now have been a Free State within the American Union, the first trophy of legitimate popular sovereignty, and a great national party with Stephen A. Douglas at its head would have been existing and triumphant, standing upon firm constitutional ground, knowing no North and no South, but regarding and protecting equally the constitutional rights of all the States.

But it was not at once so to be. Mr. Buchanan and Southern statesmen of ultra views, aided by a few Northern politicians, were infatuated enough to suppose that the two-edged sword of popular sovereignty that was sheathed[Pg 46] in the Kansas bill, was to be wielded by the Federal administration, and not by the people of Kansas, and made to cut but one way and that way in favor of slavery. And they were equally infatuated when they found that they could not force upon the people of Kansas the fraudulent Lecompton Constitution, to suppose that the power of self-government, which had been conceded to the people of the territories, could be nullified by the dogma of the sovereignty of the Supreme Court.

Mr. Buchanan and his compeers should have known before they passed the Kansas bill, that when the people of an American State or territory once laid their hands upon the power to form and regulate their domestic institutions in their own way, they held the power upon which free institutions and slave institutions alike rested in the American States, and that that power and its free exercise could never be taken from the people by any Supreme Court or the dogma of any political party, and any systematized attempt to take it away would be met by resistance that would shiver the Union to fragments. The sovereignty of the people or true democracy, like the elements of fire and water, is a gentle and a genial thing, when the hand of representative government rests kindly upon it, but if that hand dares to essay a wrong, then will the power of the people become like the burning lava of the volcano, when its pent-up fires escape, or the resistless waves of the ocean, when the storm moves over its depths. The courts may guide and direct and check the popular will, but when a great political idea, like that of the rightful sovereignty of the States, either in the Union or in the territories, has taken root and settled into a well-defined opinion in the popular mind, the courts must let it alone; it is for them then to follow the popular will, not to lead it. Law is the voice of the people. Let the courts that assume to be the oracles of the law, see to it that they mistake not the people's voice, especially on those great political questions that touch the fountains of a nation's life.

The attempt of Mr. Buchanan's administration to force[Pg 47] slavery upon Kansas by means of the Lecompton Constitution, against the real sentiment of the people, and against the true intent and meaning of the organic law of Kansas, and failing in that, the attempt to override the principle of popular sovereignty, by means of a false construction of the Dred Scott decision, roused to renewed zeal and combined all the Northern elements of opposition to slavery, and in the excitement of angry passion that has followed, the great compromise of 1850, and the true character of that measure, and its legitimate consequent, the erasure of the Missouri compromise line, have been obscured in the public mind, and both have lost their hold upon the calm judgments of the people. Why is this? Are not the laws that now stand upon the statute book of the nation, as the compromise measures of 1850, the same as they were in 1852, when they were endorsed by nearly 3,000,000 of votes—almost the unanimous vote of the nation? Is the law of the Kansas and Nebraska act, annulling the Missouri compromise line, a different law from what it was in 1856, when it was triumphantly sustained against Fremont and the Philadelphia platform? No man can say the laws are not the same. As they were then, so are they now. If right in principle and good then, they are equally right and good now. Were the people senseless or did they mean nothing when they endorsed those laws? No man dare say that. Why is it then that the Democratic party, which triumphed in 1852 and in 1856 on these very measures, is now a divided and broken army and almost panic-stricken, and its opponents, the advocates of Congressional prohibition of slavery, with a man at their head without a record as a statesman and almost unknown to the nation, carrying in their train all the fiercest elements of anti-slavery agitation, are already boasting of sure success? No satisfactory answer can be given to these questions, except the fact that the administration of James Buchanan, false to the principles on which it was placed in power, has attempted by intervention in favor of slavery, to destroy the very principle which is the life of the compromise[Pg 48] of 1850 and of the Kansas and Nebraska law of 1854. Those great measures and their ablest and most consistent champion, have alike been stabbed in the house of their friends. By the course of the Buchanan administration, the people of the North have been made to believe that the principle of non-intervention is a sham; that the compromise of 1850 and the erasure of the Missouri line in 1852 were fraudulent schemes to cheat the people into a consent to extend slavery all over the national territory; and the cry is echoed all through the North: the nation's plighted faith is broken, the landmarks of freedom are removed, the barbarism of slavery will spread over the land! Is there reason in this cry, for argument it cannot be called? There is none. Why the very fact that the acts of the Federal executive have had power to produce this strange delusion and wild commotion of the public mind, is itself a potent argument for holding fast to the principle of the compromise of 1850, and rallying the people again to its support, so that the President and the Congress may no longer disturb the people by tampering with the local question of slavery. Again I say, there is nothing in this cry of the extension of the barbarism of slavery; it is as senseless as it is dangerous to the nation's peace. All that is is done by the legislation of 1850 and 1854, is to establish a governing principle in regard to slavery in the territories, which is exactly the same as the principle which governs slavery in the States under the Constitution. The laws of 1850 and 1854 plant slavery no where, nor do they extend it any where into the national domain. They leave the national territory *free*.

What better authority can we have on this point than that of Henry Clay, whose influence perhaps as much as that of any other man, helped to carry the compromise of 1850? Did he mean in voting for that compromise, by which the principle of non-intervention was adopted as to territory both North and South of the Missouri compromise line of 36 deg. 30 min., to extend slavery into such territory? Hear what he said on the question in the Senate of the[Pg 49] United States. He said in answer to a demand of Jefferson Davis for a positive provision for the admission of slavery south of the Missouri compromise line:—"Coming as I do from a Slave State, it is my solemn, deliberate and well-matured determination that no power—no earthly power—shall compel me to vote for the positive introduction of slavery either south or north of that line. Sir, while you reproach, and justly too, our British ancestors for the introduction of this institution upon the continent of America, I am, for one, unwilling that the posterity of the present inhabitants of California and New Mexico shall reproach us for doing just what we reproach Great Britain for doing to us. If the citizens of those territories choose to establish slavery, I am for admitting them with such provisions in their constitutions; but then it will be their own work and not ours, and their posterity will have to reproach them and not us, for forming constitutions allowing the institution of slavery to exist among them." In the same paragraph, Mr. Clay further says, "I believe that slavery no where exists within any portion of the territory acquired by us from Mexico." So much for the testimony of Henry Clay! Now, who shall say that the compromise of 1850 was a law to extend slavery over the free territory covered by it? and if not, then for the same reason, the Kansas and Nebraska act was not a law for extending slavery over the free territory north of the Missouri line. What the law of 1850 did for the territory acquired from Mexico, the same did the law of 1854 do for the Louisiana territory acquired from France. No man can show a substantial difference, except that the Kansas and Nebraska law more clearly recognizes the right of the people to decide the question of slavery. Again, I would ask of the men who make this cry of the extension of slavery, to answer in candor: If the Missouri line was a landmark for freedom, was it not also a landmark for slavery? Was not the country south of 36 deg. 30 min., under the law of March 6th 1820, as impliedly devoted to slavery as the country north of it was to freedom? Up to 1848, when[Pg 50] California, to which northern men had been led, not more by the love of freedom than by the lust of gold, had declared herself a Free State, had a Free State ever been made south of the Missouri line? Was it not the almost sure result of that line to prevent men who favor Free States from going south of it to demonstrate by experience that Free States could grow and prosper even in a southern clime? Had free labor a fair chance to raise its standard in the south, and try its strength beneath a burning sun, so long as Congress had virtually doomed the land of the south to slave labor, by declaring that the region of free land and free labor was north of the Missouri line? Is it not slavery rather than freedom that needs the protection of positive law? Does the north, guarded as it is by nature's irrepealable law, and by the self-poised and self-reliant strength of its freeborn sons, need the Federal power to guard its soil from the feet of slaves? Is slavery more progressive and expansive than freedom? and are the men who form Free States afraid to meet the men who form Slave States on common ground and take an even chance for control? In a word, do the men who build up free institutions need any thing more from the Federal government than that it should place in their hands the ax and the sword of democracy, and let them alone?

It is astonishing to me that men who profess the sentiments expressed by conservative men of the Republican party, if they are sincere in their desire that slavery should die out, should fail to see that the compromise of 1850 and the Kansas and Nebraska law are alike based upon the only principle by which the ultimate extinction of slavery on this continent must take place. All that freedom needed, and all that it could constitutionally claim, was the withdrawal of the national intervention in favor of slavery, which intervention existed so long as a geographical line marked out by Congress existed over the national domain to separate Free and Slave States; and the leaving of the question of slavery to the local legislatures; by them only had it been or could it be created, and by them only[Pg 51] had it been or could it be abolished. When the national territory was made free by the law of non-intervention, slavery was left entirely to the local law, and as freedom is the rule and slavery the exception, the chances were three to one in favor of free institutions in every new State.

And yet it is for bringing the slavery agitation to this result—a result of which the men of the South upon their own principles cannot complain, and of which their best men do not complain, and of which the North has no reason to complain, but rather to rejoice, that Stephen A. Douglas, the ablest statesman of whom this nation can boast since the mighty intellect of Webster ceased to speak in words of power, has been covered all over with the vilest and bitterest denunciation—denunciation that would seem to be more the outpouring of personal malignity than the voice of mere partisan hostility. It is for this result that Douglas has been outlawed by a professedly Democratic administration, and the Democratic party itself broken up by Southern disunionists, aided by that same administration. But a nation's returning justice will yet lift aloft her scale, and Stephen A. Douglas can afford to abide his time.

I have thus, I fear tediously to you, brought you to the last act of the great national drama of slavery agitation.

Let us now briefly review the ground, sum up the points, and see how we stand for the final struggle near at hand.

These are the propositions I have aimed to establish:

1. Slavery existed in all the States of the Union when it was formed, and no power was conceded to Congress, under the Confederation to interfere with it.

2. The Jefferson ordinance of 1784, the first act of Congress relating to the territory of the United States, conceded to the people of the territories as inchoate States, full power of internal legislation, and did not prohibit slavery.

3. The Dane ordinance of 1787, applied only to territory not adapted to negro slave labor; it was adopted under an implied power, if any, in the Congress of the Confederation. Viewed on strict constitutional grounds, it was a usurpation, like many other powers exercised by the old Congress,[Pg 52] but it was in terms a compact more than a legislative act, and as such by consent of all the States concerned, became binding on the government and the States under the Constitution. It is, therefore, no precedent for mere legislative acts of Congress, prohibiting or permitting slavery in any territory.

4. The Constitution, like the Union itself, is the result, as declared by its framers, of "a spirit of amity and of mutual deference and concession." It recognizes slavery as a lawful institution under local law, in the basis of representation and taxation—in the right to continue the African slave trade until 1808, and in the right to reclaim fugitive slaves; but it concedes to Congress no express power to establish, or to prohibit, or abolish slavery in the States.

5. The territory acquired by the Federal government, has been acquired under the power to admit new States. The end of acquisition was to make new States, not colonies nor provinces. Hence, whether the power in Congress to govern such territory is derived from the power to make needful rules and regulations concerning the territory or other

property of the United States, or the power to admit new States, or any other express power, the power must be exercised with reference to its only legitimate end, the formation and admission of new States, in all respects of internal sovereignty equal to the original States; and the Constitution rightfully interpreted therefore, requires Congress to do no more as to legislation for the territories than to provide for territorial governments, through which the people may form and regulate their own internal affairs, subject only to the Constitution of the United States, and to admit them as States whenever ripe for that event. The object of providing territorial governments is to enable the territorial people to exercise self-government, and if fit for it as to one class of domestic institutions, they are fit for it as to another; if fit to define the relations and rights of husband and wife, of parent and child, of guardian and ward, they are equally fit to define them as to master and servant.[Pg 53]

6. If there be precedents in the action of Congress for prohibiting slavery, there are equal precedents for permitting it or extending it. Slavery was extended by acquiring Louisiana and Florida; it was extended by admitting Kentucky, Tennessee, Alabama, Mississippi, Louisiana, Missouri, Arkansas, Florida and Texas as Slave States; and the history of the Federal government in regard to slavery shows that the power of Congress to prohibit slavery has been exercised as to territory not adapted to slave labor, and the power to permit it has been exercised as to territory adapted to negro slave labor, and the criterion by which the question of prohibition or permission has been determined, has been the wants and consequent wishes of the white people of the territories. The whole question, therefore, resolves itself into the consent or non-consent of the local authority; and herein lies the absurdity of both extreme sectional dogmas of Congressional power to prohibit and Congressional power to permit, both conceding ultimate

power in the State legislatures to establish or prohibit slavery, and denying it to the territorial legislatures, in the face of the admitted fact that it is not the Congress, but the local authority that must ultimately decide.

7. Assuming that there is in Congress a discretionary or sovereign power to govern the territories, sound policy requires such government to be administered in that "spirit of amity and mutual deference and concession," in which the Constitution itself was conceived and adopted; and the absolute prohibition of slavery in all the national territory in which Free States and Slave States have a common right and common interest, is in direct conflict with the spirit of the Constitution.

Lastly—Compromise is demonstrated to be the principle of the Constitution and the policy of the Federal government in regard to slavery. A Congressional geographical line is not the true mode of compromise, as such a line implies the right of slavery to exclusive possession on one side of the geographical line, and is therefore in favor of slavery and against freedom. The question as a constitutional[Pg 54] one, is not a question between freedom and slavery, but a question of constitutional authority, growing out of the clear and fundamental distinction in the Constitution, between the powers of legislation for local or domestic purposes and the like powers for national or Federal purposes. The true principle of compromise on the part of the Federal government is neutrality, non-interference, non-intervention, or the leaving of the question to be fairly determined in the local jurisdiction where it arises. A geographical line is arbitrary and not adapted to varying circumstances or events; the principle of local sovereignty involved in that of national non-intervention, is self-adjusting and of universal application; it applies to all cases and all times, and is in itself, the only principle consistent with the theory of the government, which is that the people of each State and community have the right and capacity to regulate their own internal affairs, subject only to their respective fundamental laws or Constitutions of government and to the nation's organic law. This principle was the basis of the compromise laws of 1850, and of the erasure of the Missouri line in 1854, and has been endorsed by large majorities of the people both North and South.

Now, how do the parties and candidates seeking from the people the power to control the Federal government, stand on this great subject that divides the nation?

I shall not presume to weary your patience by dwelling on this question. Men who read and think with calm unbiased minds, cannot fail to see how they stand.

I have now only to say:

1. Looking to the men who formed it, and who lead it, the platform on which it stands, and the end which it contemplates, I regard the organization headed by Breckinridge and Lane as essentially a sectional slavery extension party, bound through the Federal judiciary, backed by the Federal government, to extend slavery into all the territories of the United States, with or without the assent of the people, and if need be to accomplish this end, bound to legalize slavery under the Federal Constitution in every[Pg 55] State of the Union, and to open the floodgates of the African slave trade under the protection of the national banner. This is the logical end of the Breckinridge and Lane platform. Its practical end will be the destruction of the American Union, for no man in his senses can believe that the Federal government, either through its President, or its Congress, or its Supreme Court, can ever make negro slavery lawful for one hour, where the free white people of any State

will that it shall not be. If slaveholders are ever to reach the throne of national power on this continent, which the Breckinridge party are aiming to erect for them, they will wade to that throne through battle fields flowing with human blood.

This Breckinridge and Lane party holds within its bosom the rankest disunionists and most ultra advocates of the African slave trade. Its true watch cry, whatever it may pretend in the North, is "*National Slavery or Disunion.*"

With this view of the Breckinridge party, I cannot therefore say that I admired the good taste or consistency of my Republican friends, when in this city a few nights ago, they encouraged by loud applause, the virulent harangue of Jesse D. Bright, the Indiana leader of the Breckinridge faction, not I presume because they approved his sentiments, but because he abused Stephen A. Douglas.

2. Looking to the men who formed it, and who now represent it as its leading oracles, Seward, Hale, Sumner, Wilson, Chase, Giddings, Wade, Lovejoy, not forgetting John A. Andrews of Massachusetts, with his negro guard of wide-awakes, nor excepting John Brown, the martyr, nor excepting the comparatively unknown Abraham Lincoln, whom the crisis of the divided house has made famous—and looking also to the Philadelphia and Chicago platforms on which the party stands, with their logical inconsistencies, and the end which those platforms, as well as the public addresses and working machinery of their advocates contemplate—I regard the so-called Republican party, whose candidates are Lincoln and Hamlin, as essentially a sectional, slavery prohibition and slavery abolition party, bound[Pg 56] by political action, through the power of the Federal government; *first*, to prohibit slavery in all the territories of the United States; *second*, to admit no more

Slave States, and ultimately by State action and Federal action too, when the Free States have become three-fourths of the whole, and sufficiently powerful to make the Federal Constitution what they please, to abolish slavery in all the States, so that, to use the language of William H. Seward at Chicago, on 2d October instant, "*Civilization may be maintained and carried on, on this continent by Federal States, based on the principles of free soil, free labor, free speech, equal rights and universal suffrage.*" This is *the creed* of the Republican party as declared by Mr. Seward, and he affirms that it is *a positive party* that will take no more compromises in geographical lines or squatter sovereignties.

This is the logical end of the platforms of the Republican party; the practical end, following the attempt to realize the other, will be disunion, with all the dire results portrayed by Daniel Webster, when in that great effort of his majestic intellect, his defence of the American Union, he prayed that when "his eyes should be turned to behold for the last time the sun in heaven, he might not see him shining on the broken and dishonored fragments of a once glorious Union; on States dissevered, discordant, belligerent; on a land rent with civil feuds, or drenched, it may be, in fraternal blood!"

I am conscious that many Republicans, whom I esteem and respect, may object to this opinion of their party and platforms. Be that as it may, the opinion is a sincere one, and I believe can be sustained by a fair analysis of the records of Republican leaders and of the proceedings of the party.

It is vain to deny that with the masses of that party, Seward is their representative man, and that without the abolition strength, which he and Sumner, Hale, Greeley, Wade, Lovejoy, Giddings, and all that class of politicians bring to the Republican ranks, they would not have a hope of success in the North. The cohorts of abolition are the[Pg 57] Zouaves of the Republican camp. It is their enthusiasm, their fiery zeal, and intolerant hate of all southern institutions, that give the Republican party no small amount of its power. The nomination of Lincoln over Seward was a trick of expediency, like the nomination of Fremont. The real leaders of the Republican organization have points too sharply defined to be trusted as candidates before the nation. Obscure men are sought, who from their very want of being known, fail to concentrate the deadly fire that would pour upon the real leaders if shown in the open field. The Republicans are shrewd enough to know that candidates sometimes win where principles would fail; hence if you would know their principles and real leaders, look *behind*, not *on* their candidates.

3. Looking to the men who formed it, and who lead it, and to the platform on which it stands, I regard the Bell and Everett or Union party as it is called, as a very respectable and honorable party, mostly composed of men of the old Whig faith, who truly love the Union and the Constitution, and will do all they can to preserve both, and who would manage the ship of state admirably well, so long as the sky was bright, the sea was calm, and nought but fair and gentle breezes filled the flowing sails; but who would be scarcely competent to guide that noble and richly laden ship in unknown seas, amid tropic or arctic storms, or when surrounded by the pirate crafts of the African slave trade, or the wildly drifting fire ships of political abolition. In such seas, amid such storms, and surrounded by such assailants, the ship of state wants men upon the quarter deck of far reaching thought, of iron wills, of hearts that know not fear; men whom storms cannot frighten and foes cannot conquer—such men as will nail "the Union" to the mast and die ere it comes down.

Lastly, my friends—Looking to the men who now compose and sustain it, and to the platform on which it stands, I regard the National Democratic party, lead by Stephen A. Douglas—I mean the party of the people, not of the politicians—as the truly democratic and national—not sectional—party[Pg 58] of this country; a party that in the august presence of the nation and its Federal Constitution, knows no North and no South, but the Union, the whole Union and nothing but the Union, and whose motto is not *"Liberty first and Union afterwards,"* but that glorious motto, "Liberty and Union, now and forever, one and inseparable."

Firmly convinced of the correctness of my opinions on the question dividing the nation, I appeal in all kindness to the Whigs and Democrats, now ranging under Republican banners, and perhaps under the uniform of Republican wide-awakes, and I ask them, Whigs and Democrats, who alike in 1852 and in 1856 sustained the compromise principle of Congressional non-intervention with slavery: why have they changed their ground? Why do they now support a party whose real motto is "No more slave territory—no more Slave States," and whose candidates are northern sectional men only? Is that the motto, or are these the candidates for a Union in which there are North States and South States, Free States and Slave States, all equal in the house of the nation, and in the nation's fundamental law?

A fearful responsibility rests on every citizen who, by his vote or his acts, aids in the first triumph of a party whose creed and whose men are sectional. On that rock will the Union, if ever, be wrecked, and towards that rock it is rapidly drifting now.

I ask again, where does the real National Democratic party of the people, headed by Douglas, now stand on the question of slavery? I answer, and no man can truthfully gainsay it, it stands where it stood in 1840-44-48, and 1852-56. It stands where it stood in 1850, when it aided to pass the great national compromise. It stands where it stood in 1854, when to carry out that compromise to its logical results, it erased the Missouri compromise line of 1820, because *that* was not a constitutional line of national brotherhood and peace, but a legislative line of division and sectional strife. It stands where it stood in 1856, when the sectional platform and the feeble candidate of the Philadelphia Convention fell before it. It stands[Pg 59] where it will stand, with its banner of Union and national peace waving over it, until patriotic Whigs and patriotic Democrats, North and South, who in 1852 made up the 2,987,000 votes that endorsed the compromise of 1850, awaking from the delusion and misunderstanding which have gathered over that great measure of national peace, shall affirm it again as a permanent and enduring law that shall bind together the now divided house of the American Union. Then, indeed, will "the crisis" of Abraham Lincoln and "the irrepressible conflict" of William H. Seward be passed in safety, and the Union again arise and shine in the full sunlight of permanent peace.

APPENDIX:

The following article from the Fort Wayne Daily Sentinel of September, 1861, is now reprinted on account of its relation to the subject discussed in the preceding pages, and as a further exposition of the views of the writer upon the position of parties in the last presidential election. The defeat of the Breckinridge party, on the one hand, has led to its attempt in the South, by armed rebellion to disintegrate the

Republic, because its Federal power could not be used to nationalize slavery; the success of the Republican party, on the other hand, has led to what the preceding and following arguments foreshadowed as its result, the consolidation of a power in the Federal government that is rapidly undermining the glorious constitutional fabric erected by our fathers, and paving the way for a central government, sustained not so much by the free, unbought love of the people, as by the strength of its military power to crush out resistance to its authority. The times demand of every true lover of his country to read and think. "Eternal vigilance is the price of liberty." Let not the people be deceived! When the Federal government assumes the power by military or other force to blot out the sovereignty of Federal States, (a proposition already before the Federal Congress), it strikes a blow at the life of American democracy, which exists in the constitutional sovereignty of the States. When that is slain, which God forbid! over its dead body, surrounded by fields of carnage, after a perhaps brief reign of anarchy, will rise an imperial monarchial power, of whose dealings with *the people* we have no better instructor than the great teacher, "History," which is "philosophy teaching by examples." Let us take heed!

[Pg 60]

THE QUESTION TRULY STATED.

Democracy and Anti-Democracy or, the Nation vs. the States and the People.

There are three distinct antagonistic parties now struggling for the control of the national government:

1st. A slavery extension party, ostensibly headed by Breckinridge.

2d. An abolition of slavery party, ostensibly headed by Lincoln, but more truly represented by Seward.

3d. A non-intervention with slavery party, headed by Douglas.

So far as relates to any possible political action in regard to slavery, in these three grand divisions are really merged all shades of opinion from the anti-slavery fanaticism of Garrison and Gerritt Smith, to the pro-slavery fanaticism of Yancey, Garlden and Keitt.

The organization headed by Bell and Everett seems to have no distinctive principle, except fidelity to the Union. It is a party of vague outlines, and without tangible substance.

Each of the three distinct parties (as do also the Bell and Everett party) assume to stand upon the common ground of the constitution and to justify their principles and measures by that sacred instrument, "the palladium of American liberty."

1st. The Breckinridge or Southern sectional theory, claiming the Dred Scott decision as its justification, is, that slavery is a benign national institution, to be fostered and protected by the Federal government "wherever its constitutional authority extends;" and the logical sequence from the Dred Scott decision, as construed in the South, is, that this national institution involves an inviolable right of property, and is carried by force of the constitution into *all the States and Territories*, and is there to be protected by the Federal government, and this idea is entirely consistent with the Breckinridge platform adopted at Baltimore on the 28th June last. A necessary result of the establishment of this theory will be the reopening of the African slave trade.

2d. The Lincoln and Seward or Northern sectional theory, is, that slavery is a relic of barbarism, antagonistic to the principles and policy of the nation, and is to be annoyed, assailed, and ultimately annihilated by the Federal government wherever its constitutional authority extends.

To sum up the two theories in a few words:

Slavery, according to Breckinridge and his school, is a *national good*, to be encouraged and protected by the national strong arm.

Slavery, according to Lincoln and Seward, is a *national evil*, gigantic and portentous, to be combatted and slain by the same strong arm.

That the South will permit slavery to be abolished in all the States by violence or starvation; or that the North will permit slavery to be established in all the States by judicial decision or otherwise, no man in his senses believes—hence looking to the legitimate results *of their doctrines*, both the Breckinridge and Lincoln parties *are essentially disunion parties*. Constant conflict and ultimate disunion are the natural sequents of their antagonism. As neither can hope to conquer the other, the Union, the common bond and roof tree of both, must be divided and fall.[Pg 61]

3d. The Douglas or truly conservative theory, resting upon the limited powers of the Federal constitution, as a compact of confederation, among sovereign and independent States, assumes that so far as the United States, *as a Nation*, are concerned, domestic slavery is neither a national good to be protected, nor a national evil to be crushed out; it is a local domestic institution, existing at the formation of the confederacy, in all the States, "under the laws thereof," and its good or evil, concerns only the local sovereignties or people with whom it exists or may exist. The Federal government not having been ordained or established to form or control the domestic institutions of the people of the confederated States, is equally powerless to destroy or to extend slavery. Its destruction or extension must be the work of local law, not of the Federal constitution, nor of Federal law made under it.

Let us re-state the points:

The Breckinridge or slavery extension party would *nationalize* slavery, by making its existence commensurate with the obligations of the Federal constitution.

The Lincoln or abolition party would *denationalize* it, by destroying it by prohibition where it is not, and by starvation where it is.

The Douglas or non-intervention party would denationalize it, by leaving the people in the respective localities, be they States or territories, to deal with it as they see fit.

Therefore, Breckinridge would use the national government to force slavery on an unwilling people.

Lincoln and Seward would use the same power to prevent a people who may desire domestic slavery from having it.

Douglas would not use the same power, either to permit or destroy, but recognizing the right and capacity of the people to govern themselves, would leave them to decide *for themselves* as to what domestic institutions they would or would not have.

There can be no mistaking as to which of the three parties occupies the true democratic ground on this subject. To rightly decide that question, we have only to reach the central and fundamental idea of the nature of the Federal Constitution, upon which each party bases itself.

The political history of the United States, since the Confederation, shows that as well in the formation, as in the interpretation and administration of the Federal Constitution, two parties have existed, representing two different political ideas—the one, State Sovereignty—the other, National Sovereignty, or, Confederation against Consolidation; or, democratic government in *the States* against an Imperial government in *the Nation.*

The advocates of a consolidated National government, the leading mind among whom was Alexander Hamilton, were, until after the publication of the Federalist, known as the National party. After that publication, and about 1790, they took the name of Federalists. Their opponents, who favored a Federal Union of limited and clearly defined powers, in preference to a strong National Government, were at first called Federalists, but afterwards took the name of Republicans, or, Democrats. The master spirit of this party was Thomas Jefferson. Principles adverse to those of Hamilton prevailed in the Constitutional Convention of 1787. Hamilton's plan of government[Pg 62] was not adopted, and by express vote of the Convention the term, "United States Government," was adopted in lieu of "National Government," as originally proposed, to distinguish the system to be formed.

The men of the Convention were men of great intellectual power and lofty patriotism, but also men of concession and compromise, and it is not therefore surprising that their different views should be so far reflected in the Constitution, their common work, as to lead to occasional difficulty in its interpretation. The Constitution is not so clearly expressed, that he who runs may read its meaning. The wisest and best men of the nation have differed as to its true construction, and their differing interpretations are mainly the result of adherence to one or the other of the adverse principles already stated—the one aiming to amplify the jurisdiction of the Federal government by liberal or latitudinarian construction—the other aiming to limit it by strict construction.

The National, or Hamilton, school of politicians hold that the Constitution is not a compact between the States, but a system of National Government ordained and established by the People of the United States—and Mr. H. asserted "that it belongs to the discretion of the national legislature to pronounce upon the subjects which concern the General Welfare." John Adams, an ultra Federalist, in his letters to Roger Sherman in 1789, attempted to show that the Federal government is "a monarchial republic," or, "limited monarchy," and contended that the President should have been an integral part of the national legislature by being invested with an absolute veto power.

The Democratic, or Jefferson school of politicians, on the contrary, hold that the Constitution is a compact between sovereign and independent States, and the government formed by it one of strictly limited and defined powers, delegated by the States.

Among the eminent men who have adopted *the national* theory of the constitution, were Mr. Hamilton, Chief Justice Marshall, Justice Story and Mr. Webster, and to their great abilities and powers of argument, may in part be attributed the fact that the decisions of the Supreme Court of the United States on constitutional questions of a political character, have favored the national or anti democratic theory of interpretation. These great men were federalists, and no one can doubt that their general political views have given shape and color to their legal arguments and opinions.

The people, to whose welfare democratic principles are vital, have not always yielded to the opinions and reasoning of the Supreme Court, or of the Federal school of statesmen and jurists; but have gradually from time to time by their clearly expressed will in the popular elections, imposed just restraints upon the action of the Federal government. They have thus repeatedly voted down a National Bank, a high protective tariff, a national system of internal improvements, and other kindred measures, based, like the attempt to abolish slavery, upon the same constitutional theory, that the Federal government is one of general or discretionary powers; or as Mr. Hamilton expressed it, "that it belongs to the discretion of the national Legislature to pronounce upon the subjects which concern the general welfare."

The Democratic principle of limited and specific power in the Union, for Federal purposes, and general sovereignty in the people of the States, for all local and domestic purposes, has taken deep root in the minds of the people, and has received their frequent endorsement.

The Democratic party have recognized this principle in their platforms, and in the platform of 1852 at Baltimore, and in that of 1856 at Cincinnati, and in that of 1860 at Charleston, they incorporated as one of the main foundations of their political creed, the constitutional doctrines of Jefferson and Madison as expressed in the Virginia and Kentucky resolutions of 1797 and 1798 and Mr. Madison's report of 1799-1800, which are expressly opposed to the Hamilton theory of a consolidation of the States into one sovereignty, *"the obvious tendency and inevitable result of which would be*," as Mr. Madison says, "*to transform the republican system of the United States into a monarchy.*"[Pg 63]

It is beyond doubt, this democratic doctrine of the sovereignty of the people of the States which has, more than any other, given to the Democratic party its strength with the people, and enabled the States themselves to grow and prosper, while the nation, as the symbol of their united sovereignty, has made the name of "The United States," known, and honored, and feared in every land.

Accordingly, then, as theories or principles of national politics favor or oppose the consolidation of power in the Federal government, upon matters of domestic concern or internal policy, to the denial or exclusion of the power of the people of the States or territories over the same matters, so are those theories or principles, and the measures based upon them, practically favorable or opposed to true democratic principles of government.

Apply, then, this test to the Breckinridge and Lincoln doctrines, and we need not be at a loss to determine to what class of political theories they belong.

The Breckinridge and Lincoln platforms both rest upon the same idea, viz: That there is a power in the Federal government or constitution, derived from implication, not from express language, in reference to the subject matter of domestic slavery, *above the power of the people of the States or territories to control*—or, to state the point a little differently: On this one subject of purely domestic concern the Federal government is stronger than the people.

The Federal government, virtually say the Breckinridge party, must every where protect, but can no where prohibit slavery: The same government, in effect say the Lincoln party, must prohibit slavery, but can no where establish or legalize it:

True it is, that the Breckinridge party in the 3d article of their platform say: "That when the settlers of a territory having an adequate population, *form a State constitution*," the State "ought to be admitted into the Federal Union, whether its constitution prohibits or recognizes the institution of slavery;" but at the same time they so construe the Dred Scott decision as to affirm that the right of property in slaves is guaranteed by the Federal constitution, and therefore protected every where, where that constitution is the supreme law. If so, of what avail is it for a State constitution or State law to prohibit slavery? The prohibition would be a nullity under the Federal constitution.

True it is also, that the Lincoln party affirm in the 4th article of the Chicago platform, the necessity of maintaining "the right of each State to order and control its own domestic institutions, according to its own judgment exclusively;" but in the 8th article of the same platform, they affirm the right and duty of Congress, *by legislation*, to maintain the territories in their normal condition of freedom, and they deny "*the authority of Congress, of a territorial legislature, or of any individual, to give legal existence to slavery in any territory of the United States.*"

The pretense then of conceding sovereignty to the people of the States "to order and control" the domestic institution of slavery, when that sovereignty is denied to the same people while in a territory, is a piece of transparent hypocrisy. Does not any sensible man know that prohibition of domestic slavery in a territory, is essentially prohibition of it in a State to be formed of that territory? As the twig is bent by Congress in the territory, so will the tree be inclined in the State. If slavery does not exist in a State at its organization, it will never exist there, unless forced there by the Federal government under the Breckinridge construction of the constitution.

But again: If Congress, as the Chicago platform affirms, because of the provision of the Federal constitution (5th amendment) that "no person shall be deprived of life, liberty, or property, without due process of law," cannot legalize slavery in a territory, where as the Republican platform of 1856 asserts, Congress has "sovereign power," how can a State legislature, in the face of the same constitutional prohibition or principle, (as old as *magna charta*) legalize slavery in any State where such legislature has equally sovereign power? It may be answered to this question, that the Supreme Court[Pg 64] of the United States have decided that the amendment to the constitution containing the clause above quoted, does not apply to the State governments; but this answer does not cover the whole ground, for we may ask again: how can Congress, if it has no power to legalize slavery in a territory, constitutionally admit to the Union a new State formed from such Territory with a constitution legalizing slavery? Suppose, for example, such a constitution provides. "The right of the people to hold slaves is hereby declared, and such right shall never be defeated or impaired." The State constitution has no vitality, as such, until the State is admitted to the Union—the act of admission makes the constitution a law, and a law for slavery. Congress therefore in accepting such a constitution from a new State, where slavery had not before existed, as effectually legislates slavery into such State as if a special Congressional act were passed for that purpose. Consistency then, with the Chicago platform would seem to require, that Congress should refuse, for want of constitutional power, to admit any State with a slavery constitution. I here incidentally ask another question: if the constitution, as is asserted, gives Congress *sovereign power* over the territories, where is the obligation on Congress ever to permit a territory to rise above its territorial condition, and become a State, except on such terms as Congress may impose? What is constitutionally to prevent Congress from erecting and continuing territorial governments until the territories *under the sovereign power of Congress*, outnumber and overshadow the States, and the national government becomes an Imperial power, like the Roman or British Empires, with hundreds of tributary States or provinces?

I ask again: If the normal condition of all the territories of the United States is that of freedom, and if Congress cannot legalize slavery in any territory, can the Federal government bring slaves under the power of Congress by acquiring territory governed by foreign slave laws, as were the territories of Florida and Louisiana? Does the foreign slave code continue to exist *proprio vigore* in the absence of express recognition by the Federal government; or does the force of the constitution itself annul upon the acquisition of the territory, the local law of slavery, and abrogate all treaty or legislative provisions, if any, for its continuance? In other words can the Federal government, by simple act of acquisition, or expressly by treaty, legislative act, or judicial decision, enact or continue in force a foreign slave code over territory acquired by the United States, "the normal condition of which is that of freedom?" I would be glad to know what the Chicago platform means by that expression. Does it mean that slavery cannot exist in any territory of the United States over which the constitution extends? or if it does exist there by virtue of a foreign local law at the time of acquisition, does it mean that Congress can abrogate the right of property under that law and make the territory free?

If the Republican platform really means that the Federal government cannot legalize slavery by acquiring slave territory; and cannot legalize slavery in any territory already acquired; and cannot admit a State with a slavery constitution, does not the same platform drive the Republican party to the doctrine that domestic slavery *has not*, and *cannot have* any legal existence in any State or territory where it did not exist by local law when the Federal constitution became operative? What then becomes of the asserted "right of each State to order and control its own domestic institutions according to its own judgment exclusively?"

I put all these questions by way of suggestions, not assertions, and leave the respective advocates of the Lincoln and Breckinridge platforms to answer them consistently with the Union and the Constitution.

Examine them in any light to which they may be presented, the Breckinridge and Lincoln doctrines equally lead to the same anti-Democratic result:—Sovereign power in the Federal constitution and government, superior to the power of the people of the States and territories, over the domestic institution of slavery. Directly opposed to this position is the one held by Mr. Douglas; absence of power in Congress, and full power in the people of the States and territories to deal with all their domestic institutions and local affairs. Which is the Democratic position?

J. K. E.

www.ingramcontent.com/pod-product-compliance
Lightning Source LLC
Chambersburg PA
CBHW050600280326
41933CB00011B/1919